Tears Are Not Enough

The German-Jewish Reconciliation Program Faces
The Truth about the Nazi Holocaust

by

Tom Forres

Prtintland Publishers
Hyderabad, India
2008

Copyright © 2006 by Tom Forres

tforres158@gmail.com

1st Printed in the United States of America

2nd Revised Printing in India

ISBN: 81 7887 007 X

For additional information or to order additional books,
Please write or email:
T.Forres,
158/16 Holzheimer Rd., Bethania,
QLD. 4205
AUSTRALIA

Printed and Published by:
Printland Publishers*
GPO Box 159, Hyderabad AP, 500001. India

To order books or contact us please email or visit our online bookshop
Email: info@printlandpublishers.com
www.printlandpublishers.com

*Printland Publishers is the printing and paper division
of Culcreuch Exports Pvt. Ltd.

PRINTED IN INDIA

This book is dedicated to the memory of the 6,000,000 Jewish victims of the Nazi Holocaust and to all who still suffer persecution because of their race or belief.

The House Of The Wannsee Conference where in January 1942 the Nazi government made the decision to exterminate 11,000,000 European Jews

FRONT COVER

Memorial at the site of the former Levetzowstrasse Synagogue in Berlin listing 40 SS deportation transports of Jews destined for Auschwitz and other extermination camps in the East between October 1941 and April 1945. Altogether, more than 55,600 Berlin Jews were deported. Only very few survived.

The Plötzensee Memorial to the 6,000,000 Jews
murdered in the Nazi Holocaust

Tears Are Not Enough

The German / Jewish Reconciliation Program
September 2000

Introduction

PART I

The Historical Perspective

PART II

Recollections From The Past
And Hope For The Future

PART III

Reliving The Past In The Present

PART IV

The Enigma Of The Jew's Survival
Their Return To Germany And To The Land Of Israel

PART V

Some Final Thoughts On Forgiveness
And Reconciliation

PART VI

Epilogue

PART VII

Bibliography
Photo Acknowledgements
Suggested Reading

Index

PART I

The Historical Perspective
The Australian Connection

PART II

Recollections From The Past
And Hope For The Future

Index (Contd.)

PART III

The Berlin Tour
Reliving The Past In The Present

Index (Contd.)

List Of Illustrations

Acknowledgement and Disclaimer

T his book is the outcome of more than six years work which began in late in the year 2000. Initially, only five copies of a seven page leaflet with the title: *"A Visit To The New Berlin"* were released to selected readers in Germany, Australia and England. In early 2002 following suggestions for a more comprehensive report, work commenced on a lavishly illustrated 235 page manuscript entitled: *"Tears Are Not Enough -The German/Jewish Reconciliation Program faces the Truth About The Nazi Holocaust."* I believe this title is more appropriate to the subject matter and the message it conveys. Finally, in September 2006. the first copies came off the press at the American publisher. All books from the first printing were sold within six months and from August 2007, following a major revision of the text, *"Tears Are Not Enough"* is being reprinted with planned access via the Internet and *e-book* facility, and depending on demand – on CD.

Although *"Tears Are Not Enough"* was essentially compiled and produced by the author, this book could not have come to fruition without my wife Stella's continuing support. For her untiring long term tolerance and patience, I am deeply grateful. My thanks also to the late Cynthia Mace for proof reading the original manuscript, to Ralph King for his helpful suggestions relating to the 2nd Printing and to the Rosedog Book Publishing Co.Inc. of Pittsburgh,Pa.,USA for their patience during the initial publishing process. More than anything, however, this book is a tribute to the long term dedication of the Berlin Senate and its co-workers, and the personal commitment of past and present mayors, presidents, members of the German parliament, the Jewish communities of Berlin and other individuals mostly unknown to this author. These are the people who made this German/Jewish Reconciliation Program possible and continue to give their time and effort to this worthy cause. In this regard, the organiser of our group in September 2000, Herr Ruediger Nemitz and Herr Eberhard Diepgen, the former mayor of the Berlin Senate, deserve special mention. Thanks are also due to our two principal tour guides, Herr Reimar Volker and Frau Hannelore Fobo, whose dignified handling of the Jewish Memorial Sites helped to make this often traumatic experience less painful.

Although, most photos were taken by myself during the Berlin visit, others are from official publications. My thanks go therefore to the following publishers who kindly gave permission to use material and in some cases, citations from their publications. These are given credit where appropriate in the text and in the Appendix Section.

AKTUELL.-Published by the Presse und Informationsamt des Landes Berlin 2000 -Jaronverlag GmbH, Berlin

Gedenkstätte Plötzensee Memorial Centre, Berlin

J.B.Metzlersche Verlagsbuchhandlung-Carl Ernst Pöschel Verlag GmbH. Stuttgart.

Presse und Informationsdienst der Stadt Frankfurt /Main

The Christadelphian Magazine & Publishing Association, Birmingham UK.

Grove Press Books -distributed by Publishers Group West, NY, USA

Philipp Von Zabern Mainz Publishers

Despite repeated efforts to contact some other publishers, they could not be traced. This author therefore apologizes to these organisations for such omissions and would be grateful to receive any information so that future editions can be amended.

Rahmel Verlag GmbH, D 5024 Pulheim1, Falkenweg 8

Schöning & Co,Gebr. Schmidt Lübeck V Haude & Spenersche Verlagsbuchhandlung GmbH.

Berlin Diana Verlag, Munich

A comprehensive list of all publishers is given in the Appendix Section PART VII.

Tom Forres
Email: tforres158@gmail.com

Introduction

I n the years leading up to WW II, the German Nazi government
initiated a program to systematically destroy the Jewish
presence in Europe. As early as 1935, under the so-called '*Nürnberg
Laws*', all German Jews were declared '*stateless*' and deprived of their
political and personal rights. When they were later forced to leave
Germany, they were thus wholly at the mercy of foreign governments
still willing to save them. In this hour of desperate need, the British
government and people opened their hearts and doors, thereby enabling
more than 10,000 Jewish children from Germany, Austria and
Tschechoslovakia to come to England on what became known as '*The
Kindertransport*'. And so in March 1939, this author and his sister joined
hundreds of other Jewish youngsters at the Berlin Anhalter Railway
Station waiting for the train which would take them out of Germany and
to an unknown future in England. Now resident in Australia since 1966,
in September 2000, more than 61 years after leaving Germany, we
received a joint invitation from the Berlin City Authorities and the re-
established Jewish communities to visit the capital as their '*honoured
guests*' under the German/Jewish Reconciliation Program. ***"Tears Are
Not Enough"*** is an appraisal of this remarkable program and an
expression of my personal thoughts and impressions which came out of
this unforgettable week in Berlin, the City where my sister and I were
born and where we spent much of our childhood.

The German/Jewish Reconciliation Program was initially set up as a
joint venture by the Berlin City Senate and the Jewish communities more
than 25 years after the liberation of Auschwitz and other Nazi
concentration camps in 1945. The program is seen by the organizers not
only as an act of atonement, but also as a tribute to the important long-term
historical contribution made by German Jews to the nation's scientific,
commercial, and cultural life. In this act of reconciliation, the Jewish
children who had been expelled from Germany during the Nazi era were
not forgotten and for more than 30 years, the German people have sought
to rewin the hearts and minds of the thousands of Jews who as children
were forcefully expelled from Germany during the Nazi era. Since its
inauguration, this remarkable program has enabled more than 35,000 of

these former 'children', now mostly in their 70's and 80's, to revisit the capital and other German cities as *'honoured guests'* of their respective local authorities and the re-established Jewish communities. *(Aktuell 66 / 2000 p4).*

In a sense, **" *Tears Are Not Enough* "** is really a quest to rationalize the racially tolerant 'New Berlin' of today, (and indeed the German people themselves), with the trauma of childhood and the events which led to the expulsion of my own and thousands of other Jewish families from the capital sixty one years ago. In this quest for answers rooted in the past, certain *'hidden factors'* are revealed which give the program a potentially more universal application.

There is no doubt that the program's success is to a large extent due to the Senate's true understanding of the problems facing aged returning Jews, who still daily live with the trauma that was their childhood under the Nazi dictatorship. But most importantly I believe, the German/Jewish Reconciliation Program owes its success to the organisers' appreciation that atonement for Nazi crimes against the Jewish people and other minorities can never be made ' *morally acceptable'* with material gifts, nor can forgiveness be *'bought '* with legislation or political rhetoric. The program recognizes that true reconciliation between Germans and Jews has to be an ongoing process in which both parties have to play their part. The Berlin program therefore sets out to bring to the attention of every new generation, whether Jew or Gentile, that more than 60 years after the Holocaust, the world should not only *permanently* remember the terrible crimes committed by Nazi Germany and her allies against the Jewish people, but should also be aware of the continuing efforts being made in Germany today both by official bodies, and by individual citizens to mend the rift which has for so long divided Jews and Gentiles. The German/Jewish Reconciliation Program is therefore but one aspect of how this country's general attitude towards Jews and the disadvantaged in society has changed and it is to their great credit that since the end of WW II, Federal governments have not shirked from the reality of Nazi war crimes against the Jewish people and other minority groups, but have consistently continued to acknowledge these. Above all, the Jewish memorial sites erected wherever such atrocities were committed, such as the newly dedicated Berlin Holocaust Memorial in the centre of the City, *(See Page 204)* stand not only as permanent witnesses regarding the serious consequences of political non-vigilance and apathy, but also inform every new generation of the Nazi terror that was Hitler's 'Final

Solution' Program, once aimed at the extermination of all European Jews and their culture.

An important aspect of the Berlin initiative is its recognition that true reconciliation can only be achieved where respect and empathy between individual Germans and Jews has been established. Every encouragement is therefore given for personal interaction between visiting Jewish ex-refugees and German families. Not only do such personal interactions stimulate mutual trust and respect, but they create an atmosphere where both sides see each other not merely in racial or cultural terms, but as individuals and worthy human beings. Seen in this light, reconciliation becomes *'A Matter Of The Heart'*. The real impact generated by the Berlin initiative is therefore not in what it *OFFERS* in purely **material** terms to former victims of Nazi persecution, but in what it *REPRESENTS* in **moral** terms to the world. Undoubtedly, because of its well established success, this program has much to offer to other countries aspiring to a better understanding between peoples of diverse ethnic background and cultures.

Because I believe this potentially wider application of the German initiative may also have relevance in Australia, where the question of reconciliation with the Aboriginal people is still a matter of ongoing public concern, a historical section has been included in this book on *'The Australian Connection'*. We see here not only some important parallels between the British *"White Australia Policy"* since the arrival of the First Fleet in 1788 and the Nazi persecution of the Jews in Germany, but the report also highlights the different historical influences which have over time shaped the German and Australian approach to reconciliation.

"Tears Are Not Enough" then is far more than a mere review of a city bus tour to visit Jewish memorial sites and places of cultural interest. The primary purpose of writing about the Berlin initiative was to 'look behind the scenes' and reveal those factors which lie *'hidden'* within the program itself. These are discussed at length in the closing sections of the book. As will be seen, the motivational forces which drive the German/Jewish Reconciliation Program, are in fact an expression of the new spirit within the German people themselves and their current attitude towards the growing presence of Jews and other minorities in their country. (*See speech by the former Bundespresident Roman Herzog, Page.xvii)*

Considering Germany's violent anti-Semitic past, it is remarkable indeed that Jews returning to Germany, have generally received widespread acceptance by the public and that this should have occurred at a time when the German government and its people are facing ongoing problems with immigration of refugees from various Eastern European, Asian and African countries. As a result of this public tolerance, many repatriated Jews and other legal refugees have over time assimilated well into the Federal Republic and are again making a positive contribution to the national way of life.

The Berlin program is therefore but one aspect of Germany's ongoing reconciliation initiative and its long term benefits are likely to be felt not only by the growing Jewish communities but also by other ethnic minorities within the Federal Republic. Undoubtedly, the program also represents an important milestone in Germany's bid to be seen by the world as a democratic leader in today's cosmopolitan Europe. But beyond this, by its very existence, as well as by its long standing success, this unique program sends a powerful message of hope to *all* politically oppressed minorities who still suffer persecution because of their race or belief. Furthermore, governments confronted with the problem of racial and religious diversity, can now review their existing strategies in terms of the German model. Central to the program's *'pathfinder'* role is Germany's acceptance at the highest political level that an 'admission of guilt' by the former aggressor <u>must</u> be the first step on the long road towards true reconciliation. ***"Tears Are Not Enough"*** – *the German/Jewish Recon-ciliation Program Faces The Truth About The Nazi Holocaust"* is testimony that in contrast to other countries responsible for crimes against humanity during WW II (and since), the German people and their governments have shown consistent moral courage and political will to accept their responsibility for the greatest crime in recent history. At a time when denial of the Nazi Holocaust is again on the increase, Germany's persistent determination to remember its own criminal past, is her assurance to the world that "never again shall Germans be responsible for such a tragedy".*(See comments by former Berlin Mayor, Page 44).* ***"Tears Are Not Enough"*** then is as much a tribute to those Jewish Holocaust survivors, who in the twilight of their years had the courage to go back to the land of their birth, there to relive the trauma of their childhood, as it is to the German people themselves - for without the combined effort of both Jews and Gentiles, the German/Jewish Reconciliation Program would not have survived.

THE SPIRIT OF THE NEW GERMAN/JEWISH
RELATIONSHIP

Extracts from a speech by the former German Bundespräsident Dr.Roman Herzog addressing the Berlin Bundestag in 1999 on the 54th Anniversary of the National Holocaust Remembrance Day, commemorating the liberation of Auschwitz Concentration Camp on January 27th 1945. In his speech, the president refers to the permanent National memorial to be erected in Berlin, in memory of the 6,000,000 Jews murdered by the Nazi government during the years of the Holocaust. After many years of deliberations between German and Jewish consultative organizations, the memorial was finally inaugurated in May 2005. The sentiments expressed by the President reflect the post-war German Spirit of Tolerance and Respect not only towards Jews but also other minorities within the Federal Republic.

Extract: *" The pain and suffering one section of mankind can inflict on another, is today deeply burnt into the consciousness of every German as well as into the consciousness of our nation as a whole. This day, which recalls the liberation of Auschwitz and other concentration camps, serves as a permanent reminder of this event in 1945. The question today is not so much whether we should remember, but rather what form a permanent memorial should take. This question is especially relevant in our present society, because the majority of Germans today have not in themselves experienced the National Socialist era and its crimes".*

"New generations have emerged, and for them, any connection they have with that period of German history can only be in the form of 'relayed' information regarding the Nazi era, not through personal experience. This means, in any discussion today regarding National Socialism, there is a difference in understanding and interpretation as perceived by succeeding

generations and this brings with it a danger to condone rather than to condemn the past and its crimes. This has important consequences. For instance, it is no longer possible for either the post-war generation with its ongoing responsibility or the present generation of grandchildren to detach themselves from the events of the past by adopting an attitude of moral superiority. Looking at the situation in retrospect, Germans living today can no longer pretend to take the side of the innocent Nazi victims or the resistance fighters on the one hand, and at the same time look down upon their political opponents as alleged followers of those who committed these crimes".

"NATIONAL SOCIALISM IS OUR COMMON AND MOST TERRIBLE INHERITANCE ."

"But, with the gradual passing of the first generation, many of whom were guilty either, because of their direct active involvement with or passive support of the Nazi system or, because they simply ' looked the other way', a new opportunity for understanding with each new generation opens now before us and this gives us great hope for the future."

Referring to the planned permanent memorial for the 6,000,000 murdered Jews of the Nazi terror, Bundespräsident Roman Herzog continues:

"We Germans must erect this memorial as a warning,, as a demonstration of our self esteem and determination; It is not only there for the world to see, neither should it be regarded as an eternal admission of our guilt, nor as a cheap or even morally dishonest attempt to identify ourselves with the victims. This memorial must be what its name implies – not only a permanent reminder of the terrible crimes which were committed, but most importantly, a memorial to the victims and their suffering and a warning to the living. The great majority of Germans living today are not personally responsible for the horror that was Auschwitz. But of course, in a very special sense, they too have to bear a responsibility – for it is now their duty to ensure that nothing like the Holocaust and Auschwitz can and will ever again be repeated. Furthermore, the vast majority of Germans today are not responsible for the Nazis' racial selection process, the deportations and mass murder. But again, all Germans have a special responsibility to ensure that wherever they may be called upon to speak on global issues, they will neither condone nor excuse these kinds of crimes. This applies in particular

to anti-Semitism. Although, no more prevalent in Germany at this time than elsewhere, any desecration of Jewish graves in this country must engender in us a greater sense of revulsion and resistance than when such incidents occur abroad. In no way must anti-Semitic activists be allowed to take root again in this country.* We must therefore be eternally vigilant to detect any incidents of 'segregation' or discrimination on the grounds of ethnic origin, religion or any other pretext for persecution. Even anti-Jewish remarks or so-called' racial jokes', no longer have a place in our society".

"During the last 50 years, a new German society has emerged which would have seemed impossible to envision at the beginning. Certainly, we do not yet have the ideal State. But, we have developed in this country a basis for tolerance and freedom; we have created a democratic society, a national constitution based on justice; we have created opportunities for the individual to reach his or her maximum potential; we have a high degree of social security and freedom of speech and the press. All these are of benefit to the community as a whole and an achievement pleasing to all. And most importantly, every one of these post-war developments which form the basis of our social interaction, stand in direct contrast to everything which identified the era of National Socialism. This is the Germany of today as seen and respected by the rest of the world. The German nation is seen today – as the defender of justice and supporter of human rights, an advocate for freedom of the individual and protector of the weak. And this – not political niceties, is what I hear in all the countries I visit. And this is how it must continue! Of course all these questions also have a futuristic application, but that does not give us the right to gloss over the past – for nothing gives us that right – neither the victims of the Nazi Holocaust, nor above all, our overall responsibility for the future of mankind..

---

* Speech is taken from AKTUELL 63/1999 p.31-33 and reproduced with kind permission from the Presse und Informationsamt des Landes Berlin.

(Translation by the author)

Note:* It is interesting here to recall an incident reported on the Deutsche Welle TV News program in December 2006. In the North German City of Oldenburg, a neo-Nazi group was bidding for possession of a certain building. But the citizens of the town, supported by the Mayor, were determined to prevent this and held massive demonstrations and fund raising activities to collect enough money to buy the premises, thereby thwarting any attempt by the neo-Nazi group to establish themselves in the town of Oldenburg.

Ceremony at the Berlin Grunewald Station commemorating the 55,696 Jewish men, women and children who started their final journey from here to Auschwitz and other Nazi death camps in the East.

PART I

The Historical Perspective
The Australian Connection

Two German Jewish families at a family gathering before the war.
Only two people in this group survived the Holocaust.

The Trauma of Nazi Persecution

W hen one is privileged to experience a 'once in a lifetime' event, it is appropriate that this should be recorded for the benefit of others who have not been so fortunate. Our visit to Berlin as the invited guests of the Governing Mayor and the Jewish communities was certainly such a memorable occasion. Except for a short one day visit in 1993, it was the first time my sister and I had been back to the city since our expulsion in March 1939 and as expected, the visit brought back many memories of the past. As the airport bus entered the city, I recalled how as a 12 year old, I stood on a cold, bleak morning in March 1939 with my sister and mother at the Berlin Anhalter railway station with hundreds of other Jewish children, waiting to board the *"Kindertransport"* train which was to take us to an unknown future in England - strangers in a strange land. When, sixty one years later, we again passed some of Berlin's famous landmarks, old memories came flooding back, and soon the distinction between present day reality and the time of our turbulent childhood became increasingly blurred as past and present merged together to create new experiences. It felt strange indeed to have been part of that historic era and to be back once more in Berlin where it all happened - this time not as a 12 year old boy in daily fear of persecution, but as a 73 year old pensioner from Australia, the honoured guest of the Governing Mayor, the Berlin City Senate and the re-established Berlin Jewish communities.

The 46 ex–Berlin residents in our group came with their partners or relatives from the United States, Australia, Israel, United Kingdom, Canada, Argentine, Chile, Brazil, Uruguay and South Africa. The reason for this diversity is the traumatic situation in which Jews found themselves in pre-war Germany when Nazi persecution forced thousands of Jewish children to be scattered like autumn leaves across the globe to find refuge in any country still willing to save them. It was a time when Jews in Germany and Austria were fighting daily for their very existence and the primary concern of all families was to save the children.

As foreign countries which had earlier offered asylum, either closed their doors or reduced their immigration quotas, many Jewish parents were faced with a terrible 'life or death' decision. This was the awful reality that the only chance for their childens' survival, and hence the continuance of the family name, was to deliberately tear the family apart and send the children to different parts of the world where they would grow up apart in countries with diverse languages and cultures. But as so many times in Jewish history, it was in fact their dispersion which also became their means of survival. And so, whereas thousands of Jewish children were saved from the terror of the Holocaust, many of their parents left trapped in Germany, were later deported and subsequently perished in the death camps.

Whilst some siblings growing up in different continents lost contact altogether, others progressively lost their ability to communicate in their native German as they grew up in isolation from each other in separate cultural worlds. As they reached adulthood and became increasingly fluent in the language of their new host country, the gradual loss of their mother tongue often made tracing their brothers and sisters in other lands difficult and this sometimes led to the tragic situation that even when such siblings did eventually meet in later years, their only means of communication was through an interpreter. When these same '*children*', now in their 70s and 80's, come to Berlin and other German cities year by year from every corner of the globe to participate in this unique German/Jewish Reconciliation Program, their multi-lingual and multi-cultural presence on German soil is a tragic reminder of their painful childhood during the pre-war Nazi era. Regretfully, the diversity of languages together with the need for privacy in a large city hotel, made it also difficult for the tour guests to become personally acquainted with other participants, especially Spanish and Portuguese speaking guests from South and Central America having generally only a limited knowledge of the English and/or German languages.

Jewish children leaving Germany on their way to Palestine

4

Why This Book Had To Be Written

R eaders of **Aktuell** * will be aware of the many letters of appreciation and reports to the organisers sent in by ex-Berlin Jews who have already taken part in this program. Although the conventional approach is to write such reports either in the form of a diary or as a straight forward account of the various events which make up the daily program, I felt that this would not adequately express my own thoughts and impressions about this '*once in a life time*' experience. As a keen listener to the Deutsche Welle News program, relayed every morning to Australia on Channel SBS, my initial enthusiasm was motivated by what I saw as a unique opportunity to verify first hand the views expressed by that program. I wanted to experience for myself, not only the alleged '*changed German attitude towards the growing Jewish presence*', but also to personally verify the validity of reports regarding German public response to violence against the Jewish population. I therefore felt that this report should go beyond merely highlighting the excellence of the program per se. Whilst for all Jewish guests, the Berlin experience is undoubtedly an unforgettable, often traumatic personal experience, for me, living in Australia, where reconciliation with the Aboriginal people is still a major issue, it had a very special significance. Even the few days we spent in the capital indicated that this already 30 year old Jewish Reconciliation Program had a potential far beyond its German application. I believe the very fact that it had been initiated by the Senate in conjunction with the Jewish communities in the capital Berlin, the one-time seat of virulent Nazi anti-Semitism, was in itself most significant and the close cooperation between these organisations has undoubtedly contributed to the program's success. Whilst, at least to some degree, its potentially universal aspects had been mentioned during our visit, I felt here were some of the more important issues to be considered.

Note * '**Aktuell**' *is a magazine published by the Senate's 'Presse & Informationsamt des Landes Berlin' in conjunction with the Berlin Jewish Communities and is sent twice yearly to all ex-erman Jews worldwide, who as children were forced to emigrate by the Nazi government.*

Whereas for all ex-Berlin Jews, the emotional impact of actually walking along the same streets trodden in childhood over 60 years ago and seeing again Berlin's familiar City landmarks must certainly be profound, for those visitors who actually endured and survived the Nazi death camps, the experience of coming to Berlin with its traumatic memories, must be a *'Living Nightmare'*.

I became acutely aware of this, when standing next to a Jewish couple from New York at the foot of the memorial (*shown on the front cover*) commemorating the transport of thousands of Jews to Auschwitz and other death camps during the war. They were the only survivors of two large families, who in 1941 had started the *'Road To Hell'* from this SS Assembly hall which had once been the Jewish synagogue where they had worshipped together with their parents. Happily, like some other death camp survivors, they met in one of the rehabilitation camps after their release from Auschwitz and eventually married, and have thus been able to share their traumatic experiences together in the bonds of love. As I watched this couple with bowed heads, deep in their own thoughts, I found it impossible to comprehend the mental anguish such victims of Nazi racial brutality must be experiencing as they stand at the foot of the memorial which recalls the time when they, together with thousands of other innocent Berlin deportees, started their *'March To Hell'* - to the extermination camps in the East. Although understandably, there was a general reluctance to speak about such personal tragedies during the Berlin visit, the sad facial expression on those survivors, who in many cases had lost their entire families in the Nazi Holocaust, said it all. For some surviving Jews, even the very acceptance of their own existence is a trauma in itself, brought about by a deeply entrenched feeling of *'self guilt'*. **"Why Me"?** This is the question many Holocaust survivors still have to come to terms with before their souls can find peace and forgiveness. As I watched some of these survivors in deep contemplation and sorrow, I realised how hard it is for those who, like myself, had been spared the horrors of the Nazi death camps, to share the grief of these now 70 and 80 year old Jewish ex-deportees, as they stand in silence at the foot of a shrine reliving their own terrible journey and that of their parents and relatives to Auschwitz or some other destination in the East. What a traumatic experience the visit to Berlin must be for them as they recall their childhood days in the City which for them still holds such sad memories. With these thoughts in mind, I knew this report would have to go beyond merely recording the daily events of the program. Here was a personal challenge to unveil what *really* lies hidden behind the program's surface – those wider implications of the Berlin initiative which, I believe, are the real hallmarks of its outstanding success. As explained in PART V, to recognise the significance of these hidden factors, is all the more important because in the final analysis, they are surely the most far reaching issues to come out of the program. Most importantly, I came to realize that this success story is not so much due to what the program *'DOES',* but *'WHAT IT MORALLY REPRESENTS'.* But more than anything, the real importance of these 'hidden' aspects, is that they reveal a potentially more universal application for the program. We see for instance that in a sense, the Berlin authorities cannot really be regarded as the sole architects of this venture because the moral driving force which initiated and maintains the program is essentially the result of a generally changed attitude towards minorities in today's German society. It is this 'moral' energy which largely drives the reconciliation process in the capital and other German cities. In no small measure, the success of the program can therefore be attributed to Germany's post-war population and their ready acceptance of the re-established Jewish presence, the support given by successive democratically elected governments, and a constitution which after WW II established equal rights for the Jewish population and other minority groups in the Federal Republic.

So, in its wider sense, the message of hope which comes out of the Berlin program can be seen as not only being applicable to the German people themselves, but to all nations of the world. There is however a historic reminder which should not be ignored! It is that as history is witness, the evils of racial hatred and religious bigotry are not confined to any one nation or section of the human race, but are deeply rooted in man's competitive nature and inherent in the very makeup of _every human society_. Given the right circumstances, what happened in Germany during the years of the Nazi era could, and has also repeatedly happened elsewhere? *(See Page 14)*. The moral transformation which occurred in Germany in the post-war period, and the lessons learnt over thirty years can I believe, also be successfully applied wherever the political will to greater understanding is driven by a belief in the dignity of man and the premise that neither race, social background or the colour of skin shall classify a person as '***minderwertig***', that is of *'no value to society'*, the term used by the Nazis to justify their extermination of Jews and other minorities.

True reconciliation must therefore be based on the acceptance by both parties that irrespective of their social or ethnic status, all men and women are created in the image of God and are of equal value in the overall well-being and progress of mankind.

The real success of the Berlin program lies in its ability to set an <u>universally</u> applicable example in tolerance and understanding. As such, it shines like a beacon of hope to all the oppressed of this world. The success achieved in a country which had for generations been steeped in the evils of racial intolerance, is their assurance that the gulf of racial prejudice

which now divides people, <u>*can be bridged*</u> – that the wounds caused by religious bigotry, <u>*can be healed*</u>. As shown in the following pages, in this crusade of mutual acceptance and forgiveness, both the oppressor and the victim have to play their part. It is therefore vital that the lessons learnt in Germany, are not allowed to disappear in the corridors of political expediency – they must become the blueprint for all nations who now seek genuine reconciliation and forgiveness with those they previously oppressed. Given the political will, the Berlin initiative can become the means to this end.

ONE WORLD

The Australian Connection and The Plight of the Aborigines

A ustralian interest in the Berlin program is of special significance because it highlights yet another important reason for writing this book. Surprisingly, there is a link between the Nazi persecution of the Jews in pre-war Germany and a 1980s policy change in the Australian education system. Whilst at first, there seems little connection here, a closer look reveals there is in fact a '*hidden*' and very relevant link.

Since the 1980's, in the drive to develop her export trade in the rapidly expanding Asian region, and with a view to maintaining political and economic stability in the South Pacific, Australia's economic interests have progressively shifted from the European sphere of influence to the Asian region. This change has been partly motivated by a public demand for an Australian Republic and an associated call for what some Australians believe to be the eventual (inevitable) severance from the British monarchy. Not surprisingly, the political ramifications resulting from such a shift in public thinking go beyond the purely commercial considerations of Australia's import/export trade objectives. One of these factors has to do with the changed language teaching in Australian schools. Where once German and French were taught, (except in some private schools), these traditional European languages have now been largely replaced by Indonesian, Chinese and Japanese. Whereas in the past, students who were taught German or French were at least to some extent acquainted with basic European history, geography and culture, under the present policy many young Australians are today growing up with little appreciation of Germany's rich cultural and artistic heritage as well as her important historical role in the development of Europe and the world during the last 200 years. This shift towards an increasingly Asian oriented climate in Australian education has occurred despite the great variety of available information in school libraries, computer programs and the Internet. The resultant limited appreciation by Australian children of European history and culture, largely the result of this changed language teaching policy, was brought out in a year 2000 survey, where only a few 14 and 15 year old senior high school students could name Sir Winston Churchill as Britain's prime minister in WW II, and the name Adolf Hitler was generally only associated with *"The Man Who Killed The Jews"*.

But it is not so much the students who are at fault, rather it is the effect of the powerful, all invasive media which today so strongly influences education and the minds of the young via the Internet and television. This lack of knowledge is therefore hardly surprising when most of the information regarding German and indeed European affairs students' receive comes from often biased and sensationalized press and TV reports of isolated incidents such as the desecration of a Jewish synagogue or the murder of a German Jew by irate neo-Nazi youths. Because of the now predominant emphasis on Asian language teaching, many young (and indeed older) Australians are not only uninformed about the historical German impact on the Arts, science and engineering, but also regarding the positive changes in the post-war German/Jewish relationship. It is this author's hope that what is written here may, at least to some extent, help to rectify this omission.

In order to understand the meaning of reconciliation in the Australian context, one has to appreciate the severe shock which the sudden arrival of Europeans in the latter part of the 18th Century had on a 40,000 year old Stone Age culture. For the benefit of readers unfamiliar with Australia's colonial history, the following historical background explanation highlights the differences and similarities between the German and Australian reconciliation programs.

Following the loss of the American colonies in 1783, the British government saw the future colonization of Australia as a welcome solution to the chronic deprivation and poverty sweeping the country as the result of industrialization during the latter part of the 18th Century. Whilst factory owners and merchants made huge profits from newly created industrial wealth, workers including children, were condemned to toil long hours in the mines and factories virtually as slave labour under the most appalling conditions. And with this social inequality came the inevitable rise in crime, leading rapidly to a grossly overloaded prison system.

A politically expedient solution to this situation was conveniently found in the exploits of Captain James Cook who in 1769 had been ordered by the British admiralty to take his ship 'The Endeavour' to the island of Tahiti in the Pacific Ocean in order to record the path of the planet Venus across the sun. After successfully completing his mission, secret government orders instructed him to find the unexplored 'Great Southern Continent'. Sailing in previously uncharted waters up the Eastern coast of Australia in search of a suitable anchorage, Captain James Cook found the ideal haven at Botany Bay, (South of Sydney). It is characteristic of the man that he deliberately set out not to be the first man to set foot on the Australian mainland but allowed one of his crew to have that honour. He then. planted the British flag on the beach and '*In The Name Of The King*' took possession of the land. Cook's vital discovery of *"The Great Southern Continent'*, quickly convinced the London elite that a foothold on the Australian mainland would not only provide a welcome solution to the bulging prison population in England, but would also greatly strengthen British naval and commercial power in the Pacific and the Asian region. On his return to England, Captain James Cook persuaded the government that Port Jackson (now Sydney), north of Botany Bay, would be a suitable location for the setting up of a primary penal colony on the Australian continent. Approved by Parliament in 1776, (the year of the American Declaration Of Independence), the first fleet arrived in 1788 carrying 568 men and 191 women and child convicts and a large contingent of soldiers. Following the establishment of the Port Jackson colony in New South Wales, other convict settlements at Hobart, Port Arthur and Sarah Island in Van Diemens Land (Tasmania), and later in Queensland, Western Australia and Victoria soon followed. South Australia was the only State which did not have a penal settlement. In the early 19th Century, further convict colonies were established on Norfolk Island in the Pacific and elsewhere. The treatment of prisoners in all these detention centres was exceptionally severe, brutal floggings were a daily occurrence, and even minor offenders convicted of no greater crime than stealing a loaf of bread, were subjected to the most brutal punishment.

For many years, the interior of mainland Australia remained unexplored, but following various expeditions towards the North and West, in 1826 the entire continent was declared a *' British Crown Colony'*, thereby laying the whole of the Australian continent open to European colonization and exploitation. Early penal settlements had to be largely self-sufficient, and because of a severe shortage of skilled labour, new settlers often had to resort to using convict tradesmen. As settlements grew, this labour shortage soon prompted a steady flow of migrants from Britain and other European countries to come to Australia, seeking their fortune first in the young colonies and later in the newly discovered gold fields rapidly opening up in many areas of the continent.

During the early stages of settlement, there were some official attempts to relocate tribal communities, but under the pressures of colonization, this policy had only limited success. As the penal colonies became more established, convict prisoners who had completed their role in the early days of settlement by influencing Aborigines to convert to the Christian faith. However, it is hardly surprising that progressive incursion into sacred ancestral lands soon led to strong native retaliation. Despite often fierce resistance, in the battles which followed, natives armed only with Stone Age weapons were no match for police and British colonial troops equipped with muskets (rifles) and other weaponry. There is no doubt that the cruel treatment of the Aboriginal people by the British military and the continued forceful acquisition of tribal lands by the occupying powers and new settlers, were essentially motivated and driven by a British *'Whites Only'* policy to settle the new continent at any cost. It was therefore clear from the start that any confrontation with local tribes protesting European land claims would b ct prisoners who had completed their sentence were encouraged to establish e met with the utmost force by the British authorities. Records show Police and troops sometimes behaved with absolute barbarity, and it was not uncommon for soldiers to alleviate their frustration and boredom by hunting down defenceless natives *'just for sport'*. Law enforcement was especially severe in Tasmania where British occupation eventually led to the extermination of the *entire* indigenous population on the island, estimated at the time to be about 2500. The last remaining pure Tasmanian Aboriginal woman died in the 1960s. But, as more and more settlers occupied native lands, the subsequent progressive decline of Aboriginal tribes was not only due to colonization. A major factor in their decline was also the spreading of Influenza, venereal and other diseases brought in by European settlers, against which the native population had no immune protection. It is therefore against this historical background that today's success and/or failure on the difficult road towards true reconciliation between the Australian Aboriginals and a strongly Western based white society has to be seen.

Disputes over land claims frequently arose because newly arrived European settlers generally had little understanding or respect for the simple Aboriginal way of life, or the importance of ancestral worship and tribal mysticism in their culture. Irrespective of where they lived, an integral part of that culture was their close affinity with the land and respect for the environment. For more than 40,000 years, (some authorities even suggest 100,000 years), Australia's indigenous people had lived in perfect harmony with their natural habitat and everything this provided. Most importantly, all tribes regarded animals and plants, their only food source, as *'sacred'* and killed only to survive. The concept of either *'owning'* or *'exploiting'* the land for economic gain, as was the ambition of settlers, was therefore totally foreign to them. And it is this conceptual difference between the deep seated Aboriginal belief in the sanctity of the natural environment on the one hand, and the economic ambitions of large pastoral property owners and mine developers to exploit the land for its natural resources and financial profit on the other, which still today lies at the very root of the ongoing debate for reconciliation with the original owners of this vast continent.

Even the founding of the Australian Commonwealth in 1901 did little to improve the lot of the indigenous population – in fact some of their worst deprivation, such as the saga of the so-called *'Stolen Generation'* followed, based on the already well established *'White Australia'* policy.

A closer look at the conditions imposed on Aboriginal people, reveals many similarities between what happened in Australia during British colonial rule and the treatment of Jews in Nazi Germany. In both instances, draconian laws were introduced to deprive the victims of their constitutional rights, a ruling which in Australia was not rescinded *until 1967*. The injustices suffered by Aboriginal people first by the *'White Australia Policy'*, and then by the *'Stolen Generation'* were part of a deliberate government strategy, even up to the 1960's, to forcefully integrate selected individual families into Western based Australian society. To this end, native children were removed from their parents and brought up in Christian mission stations or state orphanages. Because of the generally destitute conditions of Aboriginal communities, it was not unusual for native mothers to hand over their children to the authorities *'voluntarily'* in order to save them prolonged suffering. To further this racial integration process, British authorities removed and later destroyed evidence of the children's' former relationship with their tribal ancestry. Although this attempt at integration was officially portrayed as an *'Act of Mercy'*, allegedly *"necessary for their own good to further the assimilation of the Aboriginal people into the 'more sophisticated' white society"* - the reality was far different. Partly due to their ill treatment by the police and military, but also because of settler transmitted diseases and poor health services, the long term combined effect of the *'Stolen Generation'* and *'White Australia'* policies invariably resulted in the progressive decline of tribal communities and their traditional life style. And with that slow demise, much of their 40,000 year old culture was gradually lost. For altruistic, as well as commercially motivated tourism considerations, great efforts are now being made to restore these unique ancient tribal customs and ritual ceremonies. Nevertheless, despite these traumatic conditions native communities suffered first under British and then under Australian law enforcement agencies, in time some Aboriginal children began to adapt to their new surroundings and reached high levels of education which in later life enabled them to pursue successful professional careers.

And the British *'White Australia'* policy was not even confined to the treatment of Aborigines. Records show that the British government followed the same policy of deliberate deceit between 1800 and 1965, when 150,000 British children, mostly from state orphanages or charity refuges were 'sent' (deported) from England to Australia as potential *'young white colonizers.'*

Before embarking for Australia, many of these youngsters were told that their parents had been killed in motor accidents and, as in the case of Aboriginal children, any reference to their English parents was secretly destroyed. On arrival in Australia, the boys were mostly sent to remote farms in the outback, where they were often treated virtually as cheap labour working up to 14 hours a day, whilst English girls generally ended up as domestic servants for the rich. This traffic in children was especially intense after WW I and in the 1950s, when British government institutions sent thousands of allegedly *'orphaned'* youngsters to Australia, leaving them with the false belief that their parents were no longer alive.. For over 40 years these 'children' kept their emotional suffering to themselves until a film *'The Leaving Of Liverpool'* dramatically revealed their hidden secret in a 1992 television program. In some cases, it was more than 50 years after they came to Australia, before these *'children'* discovered the truth about their real past and were able to reunite with their English parents.

Shocking as this official British government policy was, from a historical perspective, it would be unrealistic to imply that Britain was the only country with a colonization strategy based on *'National Prestige'* and a fanatical zeal to enforce *'White European Supremacy'*. **Far from it !** As history is witness, it is in fact the same strategy used by **all** European nations in pursuit of their own imperialistic goals. Any attempt to rationalise European conquest of other nations, must not only take into account the alleged political and military justification but also the **MORAL** implications. **Since there can NEVER be a moral justification** for attacking and exploiting a weaker nation - **whoever is the aggressor, for whatever reason and under whatever pretext** - from a **moral** point of view – **the invasion of another country is unacceptable and constitutes a crime against humanity.** The behaviour of British troops in Australia, Africa and the colonies is therefore no different to that of other nations such as France, Holland, Belgium, Spain, Portugal, Germany, Russia, Sweden, or America etc., who in the establishment of their respective empires, all committed acts of brutality against native populations. Rather, it is a sad indictment on the **whole** of humanity that when it comes to 'National Prestige' – **'MIGHT IS RIGHT'- and on that score alone -regardless of any alleged political or economic justification -ALL nations stand equally condemned**.

And, saddest of all -as we look at our world today -nothing has changed -for we witness the same policies of **'MIGHT IS RIGHT'** driven by national pride, greed and corruption being pursued by the ruling powers who at this time between them control the military and financial resources of this world.

The Slow Road To Reconciliation

W e see here then some similarities but also major differences in the German and Australian historical background to reconciliation. Most importantly, whereas Jewish persecution under the National Socialists in Germany lasted 12 years (1933-1945), the saga of the Australian Aborigines began with the establishment of the first penal colony in 1788, and continues into the 21st Century. Whilst for most Australians, the annual 'Australia Day' on January 26th, recalling the arrival of the British First Fleet in Botany Bay is an occasion to celebrate national achievement and a reminder of what it means to be Australian, for Aborigines that day is a constant and sad reminder of a painful past, rekindling their deep seated grief and resentment. Evidence of this continuing bitterness was again seen in 2006, when Aboriginal elders burnt the Australian flag in front of a large crowd outside the Sydney Opera House.

Like the rest of the world, in the decades following WW II, Australia was still recovering from six years of conflict and the emphasis in the immediate post-war period was on industrial development, rather than on the problems associated with the country's indigenous population. With the *'White Australia'* policy still in force even in the 1960's, reconciliation with Aborigines was therefore not a government priority. But, from 1970 onwards, the tide was slowly beginning to turn, as Australians became more aware of the spiritual value of Aboriginal culture and the benefits of their simple indigenous lifestyle. The time had come for a closer understanding with the original owners of this vast continent. It soon became clear however, that more than 200 years of European influence, had left their mark of mistrust and bitterness and that any dialogue with native elders would take many years and would call for a great deal of compromise, tolerance and patience on all sides. Furthermore, any serious reconciliation initiative would not only have to address the extremely complex legal implications associated with native land rights, but would also have to deal effectively with other practical issues such as –**Education, Housing, Health, Welfare and Unemployment.**

Of these, one of the most difficult problems still facing the government today is undoubtedly the question of native land claims on large outback properties, sometimes covering hundreds of thousands of hectares and claims for unrestricted access rights to ancestral burial sites on land now occupied by large, sometimes part-foreign owned mining companies. Although some progress has been made in recent years, in general, native land claims sometimes based on long standing ancestral sacred sites are extremely complex and can lead to protracted legal confrontations between tribal chiefs, large property owners, the mining companies and their legal representatives. Some of these difficulties are related to ancient tribal law and the fact that despite generous long-term financial support by federal and state governments to indigenous people, some Aborigines in remote outback localities still prefer their nomadic lifestyle and see any external authority as a threat to their traditional way of life.

But perhaps the most difficult issue regarding reconciliation, is not the claims for land rights per se, or even the lack of government funding, but the demand by certain elders for '*a separate national status*' – the insistence to be recognized as a *'separate political entity'* – in fact, "***An Aboriginal State Within The Australian Commonwealth***". It is characteristic of this attitude that wherever possible, but especially on Australia Day, the Aboriginal flag is flown in public. The concept of a separate Aboriginal state is however quite un

acceptable to the present liberal government and is in direct conflict with the official policy of "*A United Australia*", based on human rights equality for all citizens, irrespective of colour of skin and ethnic background. Multiculturism, as it is called, is deemed to be 'the future for Australia' ,a rapidly developing economy having vast natural resources and an increasing number of migrants originating from Asia and Africa, as well as non-British European and American countries. In such a democratic '*multicultural*' society (at least in theory), all citizens have equal political and social rights, an idea clearly expressed in the ***'Australian Declaration towards Reconciliation".*** And there are also other factors which make an 'Aboriginal State within the Commonwealth' unrealistic. Although many Aborigines, attracted by urban opportunities now live in cities, other pure-blooded natives still prefer to live in small, isolated communities scattered throughout

---

Note: * *For the benefit of readers unfamiliar with the **'Australian Declaration towards Reconciliation',** this is reproduced (sic) in full at the end of PART*

the continent. Furthermore, despite a common empathy with the land, there are also substantial tribal cultural differences resulting from long-term separation and the remoteness of the outback.

Undoubtedly, however, the major hurdle to effective reconciliation, is the elders' insistence for an official '*apology*' by the government on behalf of the Australian people for the wrongs committed against their ancestors, the original owners of this land. Although Aboriginal elders regard such an admission of the White Man's **'*guilt*'** as an essential precondition to the reconciliation process, in reality, and in contrast to the situation in Germany, such a demand is impractical. Because, as stated earlier, a considerable proportion of the Australian population are now migrants from Eastern European, Asian, African or North / South American descent, such citizens have no connection with the British colonial past and its negative impact on the Aboriginal people. Also, should such an official apology ever be given by an Australian government, this would undoubtedly soon be followed by a further demand for massive financial compensation, which would have to be paid for by **all** Australian taxpayers, irrespective of origin – clearly an unacceptable consideration for both government and the nation as a whole.

With such a threat hanging over the government and a population of just 20 Million, there seems little chance of an early solution in the near future. The elders' insistence in this matter therefore does little to defuse the situation and any real progress towards reconciliation in Australia as independently defined and interpreted by both sides, is therefore likely to be a slow and painful process. However, the decision in 2005 to permanently disband **ATSIC**, the ***Aboriginal & Torres Straits Islander Commission*** because of inadequate government control over funding to outback native communities as well as other reasons, may now present a fresh opportunity for a renewed dialogue with the elders. Although there is an ongoing government commitment to resolve these matters, indications are that because of the still deeply felt resentment dating back to the British colonial era, any future negotiations will have to be based on a more conciliatory approach by both sides, namely ***a more compromising attitude by the present Government on the one hand, and a less provocative approach by Aboriginal elders*** on the other. It seems therefore somewhat over-optimistic to expect an early solution to the present situation facing Australian society.

As can be seen from the above, there are some important differences between the German and Australian historical backgrounds to reconciliation. Nevertheless, despite these differences, there are also many positive developments which have helped to ease the tension. Significant, in this regard, are the periodic mass marches by both 'Black' and 'White' supporters across bridges in Australian capital cities, symbolic of the nation's desire to *bridge the gap'*, as well as important decisions relating to native land tittles. Of importance here are the so-called Marbo Treaty relating to Aboriginal land claims in Western Australia, and the official return of the famous Ayres Rock, (Uluru) in the Northern Territory to local tribes as well as the return of other substantial tribal lands in the States and the Northern Territory.

Also of significance, is the historic decision by the Sydney 2001 Centenary Committee to lead the parade commemorating 100 years Commonwealth Federation with the '*Rainbow Serpent'*, an important emblem of Aboriginal Dreamtime mythology. Such positive steps towards a better understanding reflect today's increasing public interest and support for the Aboriginal people to be officially recognized as Australia's original land owners and fellow citizens having equal rights under the constitution.

For years, displays of traditional Aboriginal arts and crafts have been major attractions in museums and Art Centres, giving both Australian and overseas visitors an unique insight into the life style of indigenous people. Their beautifully hand crafted bark paintings, boomerangs, didgeridoos, cave wall paintings and other works of art, are a never ending delight for the thousands of tourists who come to this country every year.* Furthermore, whilst some Aboriginal men and women have made significant contributions to the nation's cultural and social life, others have achieved success in Australia's political and professional world.

But it is in the sports arena, especially in international competitions such as the Sydney Olympics in the year 2000, the Athens Olympics in 2004 and The Commonwealth Games, where today many prominent Aboriginal athletes proudly represent their country in tennis, track and field events etc. And it is mainly in recognition of their sport achieve-

---

Note: * *Unfortunately much of this Artwork is now being copied and imported from China and other Asian countries to attract the growing tourist market*

18

ments, that greater public awareness and respect for the Aboriginal cause has become evident in recent years.

Another area which is earning Aborigines public recognition is their major contribution to land conservation and the preservation of endangered animal and bird species. In every State, professional groups and scientists are today actively working together with local tribes on fire and flood control, based on thousands of years of native wisdom and practice. In a land, frequently ravaged by fire, drought and floods, this accumulated knowledge of how to survive in Australia's fragile environment, is now recognized as vital for the survival of this vast continent with its unique native flora and fauna as well as for future agriculture and re-forestation management

.From what has been said, it is manifest that neither the German nor the Australian models can achieve true reconciliation between former oppressors and their victims either by legislation or political rhetoric. Nor can the 'sins of the past' be '*morally erased'* by financial or material gifts where that past still cuts deep into those who were its victims. Above all, true reconciliation has to be seen as '***a matter of the heart***' based on a genuine desire by both the former oppressor and his victims to meet each other on equal terms and in the spirit of compassion and forgiveness. Not to recognise the spiritual side of sincere atonement is to deny the power of Christian love. The road to greater understanding and tolerance is therefore inevitably a slow and painful process. To be effective, those in power must be willing to change established norms and both parties must be willing to accept compromise.

As shown by the German program, the first and most difficult step in this process is to find an appropriate blueprint for a formal expression of remorse *repeatedly addressed in public* to the descendants of those who have been wronged. Overcoming the initial reluctance to take this first step is vital for establishing confidence in the reconciliation process as a whole, and must not be seen merely as an admission of *'guilt'*. On the contrary, as in Germany, such openly expressed remorse should be recognized as a manifestation of the former oppressor's moral courage and his political strength to accept responsibility for the past wrongs committed in the nation's name. For the victim on the other hand, having received that acclamation, the first step on the hard road to forgiveness, has to be acceptance. And it is this initial *' change of heart'* by both sides which in subsequent proceedings then becomes the basis upon which mutually beneficial goals can be explored. Without such a consistently <u>repeated</u> 'official' *'admission of remorse and acceptance of guilt"*, – there can be no *true* forgiveness and without forgiveness, there can be no *true* reconciliation.

Much of the success of the German initiative can therefore undoubtedly be attributed to the organizer's fundamental understanding of these factors. The practical applications of these conciliatory principles can also be seen in many facets of German public life. Nowhere is this more evident than in the general acceptance of the re-established Jewish communities, not only at government level, but also by the German public as a whole.

The comment made to me by the Berlin Mayor, Herr Eberhard Diepgen that: " *The question of whether a person is Jewish or not, no longer has relevance in the Democratic Republic*", is therefore of special significance. But besides this acceptance of the Jewish presence, we see in today's Germany not only a strong resolve to learn from the past, but also a determination ***never to forget*** the crimes of the Nazi era, especially against the Jewish people. Here are just a few examples:

1. *Even, 60 years after the liberation of Auschwitz, there is still constant reference in the media and by dignitaries at the highest level of government to remind Germans of their shameful past in relation to the treatment of Jews and other minorities. The Memorial at the centre of Berlin to commemorate the 6,000,000 Jews murdered by the Nazi regime is the permanent witness to the world of this nation's determination not to hide, but to learn from that past.*

2. *The yearly memorial services at sites where Nazi atrocities against Jews were committed.*

3. *The ongoing close support by German authorities for the re-established Jewish communities and Jews in the Diaspora who became victims of the Nazi Holocaust.*

4. *The massive financial compensation already paid by the German government and other organisations to Holocaust survivors, their families and to the State of Israel.*

5. *The ongoing support for the German/Jewish Reconciliation Program.*

Here then we have an important milestone on that long and difficult road to forgiveness between Jews and Germans expressed at a personal as well as at an official level. The already established principles of goodwill can also be seen as a powerful example wherever a similar atmosphere of trust and respect exists and where there is a sincere desire and the necessary political will to further the reconciliation process between former oppressors and their victims. In this regard, the success achieved by the German initiative, now provides useful opportunities for other countries to re-examine their own efforts on the difficult road to greater understanding between peoples.

Whereas, the number of books written by survivors about the Nazi Holocaust is legion, certainly in Australia, little is known about the important positive changes which have occurred in the German/Jewish relationship in recent years. In *"Tears Are Not Enough"*, the reader is not only made aware of this remarkable spiritual transformation, but also in a wider sense, the focus is brought to bear on the continuing plight of the millions worldwide who still suffer persecution because of their race and/or belief.

Aboriginal Art

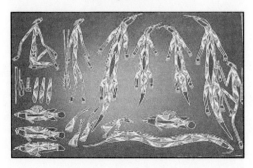

THE AUSTRALIAN DECLARATION
TOWARDS RECONCILIATION

* We, the people of Australia, of many origins as we are, make a commitment to go on together in a spirit of reconciliation.

* We value the unique status of the Aboriginal and Torres Strait Islanders peoples as the original owners and custodians of lands and waters.

* We recognize this land and its waters were settled as colonies without treaties or consent.

* Reaffirming the human rights of all Australians, we respect and recognize continuing customary laws, beliefs and traditions.

* Through understanding the spiritual relationship between the land and its first peoples, we share our future and live in harmony.

* Our nation must have the courage to own the truth, to heal the wounds of its past so that we can move on together at peace with ourselves.

* Reconciliation must live in the hearts and minds of all Australians. Many steps have been taken many steps remain as we learn our shared histories

* As we walk the journey of healing, one part of this nation apologizes and expresses its sorrows and sincere regret for the injustices of the past, so the other part accepts the apologies and forgives.

* We desire a future where all Australians enjoy their rights, accept their responsibilities, and have the opportunity to achieve their full potential.

* And so, we pledge ourselves to stop injustice, overcome disadvantage, and respect that Aboriginal and Torres Strait Islander peoples have the right to self-determination within the life of the nation.

PART II

Recollections From The Past
And Hope For The Future

The BundesKanzleramt

Centre Of The New German Democratic Parliamentary System

A Nation Spiritually Reborn
The Transformation Of Post-War Germany

I nevitably, our visit to the German capital was not only influenced by personal childhood memories, but also by the realisation that twice in a lifetime, this city had been at the centre of Germany's bid for world domination and the instigator of two world wars. The following information highlights some major events prior and during the Nazi era as well as conditions following reunification of East and West Berlin in October 1990. It is included here for the benefit of readers unfamiliar with these important periods of German history.

Following the fall of the Berlin Wall in November 1989, and the subsequent reunification of East and West Germany, a massive reconstruction program began in the newly united capital Berlin. New building sites became especially evident in areas of the former DDR, (German Democratic Republic), such as the Potsdamer Platz and the famous 'Unter den Linden Avenue' in the CBD, where after years of Soviet occupation and neglect, cranes and bulldozers could again be seen reshaping the skyline.(See Page 53). But, however significant **this** rebuilding development may have been as a symbol of Germany's material rebirth, the most important changes occurring at that time were not the extensive reconstruction programs in the capital and other cities of the former Soviet zone per se, but rather the spiritual rebirth that began to take shape in the minds of the German people themselves. The effect of this transformation was especially noticeable in Berlin capital of the Federal German Republic. Since the collapse of the former DDR and the era following reunification with the West, the City Senate (Council) has had to overcome almost impossible economic and administrative difficulties. Yet, despite this, at a time of great political and social change, the City has taken a successful quantum leap from working in a divided capital, under the former jurisdiction of both capitalist and communist administrations, to becoming the principal executive body for both East and West Berlin. Today, the German capital is the centre of one of Europe's most powerful democracies and a key member of the European Union and parliament. This City, whose name was once synonymous with the ruthless anti-Semitic Nazi racial policy, has become the very symbol of European post-war racial tolerance. Of such a track record says the Governing Mayor Herr Eberhard Diepgen in the magazine *Aktuell* (66/2000), all Berliners can be justifiably proud. This is how he sums up the progress made by City authorities since reunification in 1990:

*"The people of Berlin can look with pride upon the achievements of recent years. The physical blending (**of the two former separated sectors of the city**), is already well advanced. Without the restrictions imposed by a formal plan - without precedent - and yet in only a short time, two previously isolated parts of the City have blended together to become one. Even the life styles and relative earning capacities of Berlin citizens have become more stabilised. Common education, health and social systems have been established and the gaps which previously existed in the City traffic and communications sectors have been bridged. Increasingly, the populations in the East and West of the City are finding common ground. We have learnt from each other and with each other to overcome those problems which are divisive, so that the 40 years which once separated us, are slowly fading into the background."*

Outlining his guidelines for the future, Herr Diepgen continues:

*"In the new Century, Berlin will remain a City open to the world and will retain its international, cosmopolitan character. It is for this reason that we are especially watchful to detect any sign which might indicate an attempt to disturb the peaceful coexistence of different ethnic communities. We will pursue with the utmost vigour shameful acts, such as the desecration of Jewish synagogues and cemeteries and also any acts of aggression against the weaker members of the community and minority groups. We will show no tolerance whatever against (**racial, religious or ethnic**) intolerance. This is the challenge which both the State and the community will meet together."*

Note: *The bracketed **bold italic** comments have been added by the author to clarify the translation. (TF)*

Though ravaged by war and subsequent foreign occupation, in the years following WW II, Germany's expertise in commerce and industrial technology not only established that nation again as a major contender on international markets, but with the extensive use of foreign labour, also produced the so-called *"Wirtschaftswunder"* or "Economic Miracle" in the 1960s. At the same time as this economic upsurge and rebuilding of the nation was taking place, another, equally important development was occurring behind the scenes, namely the German peoples' changing attitude towards the re-emerging Jewish presence. With their natural propensity for efficiency, organisational skills and self discipline, once the hallmark of Prussian militarism, German authorities have over the years skilfully applied these attributes in a positive way to create a national ethos based on tolerance and equality for all minority groups in their society. The memory of two world wars with their terrible destruction and loss of life has engendered in most Germans a fierce determination that never again would this nation be responsible for such a human tragedy. It is therefore not only the political system, but also the will of the German people themselves which has, to a large extent, achieved what would only a few years ago have seemed impossible – *they have with the spirit of cooperation and tolerance changed the heart of their nation.* And this changed attitude is not confined to the capital Berlin, but was also evident in other German cities we visited like Stuttgart and Frankfurt / Main with once large pre-war Jewish populations.

One of the most important aspects of this 'transformation' following reunification has undoubtedly been the normalisation of the former East and West German education systems. The impetus behind such standardisation was to ensure that future generations of German children would no longer be indoctrinated with intolerant racial propaganda of extreme right or left wing politics, but would instead be taught the need to respect the rights of all German citizens, irrespective of religion or ethnic background. And it is after all, the need for tolerance taught at an early age, which will in later years form the basis for a better understanding of people in general and create a greater empathy for the special needs of the socially disadvantaged.

It is especially significant that the German education authorities insist on all senior students to be made aware of the political events which led to the Nazi period 1933 – 1945, especially the persecution of the Jews and the death camps. Many high schools not only teach 'racial tolerance', but even include visits to Auschwitz, Dachau and other former Nazi concentration camps in their curriculum, an experience which will undoubtedly remain with the students for the rest of their lives and positively shape their attitude towards all members of German society. Also, wherever possible, students are encouraged to talk directly with Holocaust survivors about the latter's personal experiences. There is of course a sense of urgency in this, because authorities realise that the time is coming when all Jewish survivors and eyewitnesses of the Holocaust, now in their 70's and 80's, will have passed off the scene and direct contact and dialogue with this group will no longer be possible. To further impress this policy on the German public, many special centres of remembrance and Jewish museums have been set up by city authorities to emphasize an ongoing government commitment 'never to forget'. Examples in Berlin are the Jewish Museum , opened in 1999 with its recorded 2 Millionth visitor (2004) and the extensive library and study centre at the former 'House of The Wannsee Conference', dealing specifically with the Nazi persecution of the Jews, as well as with all aspects of racial intolerance. Both venues are visited each year by thousands of German and foreign students and historical researchers from overseas. It is particularly significant that the House of the Wannsee Conference should become a venue for the study of racial <u>tolerance</u>, because it was here, that in January 1942, following a SS survey of all Jews living under German occupation, the decision was taken by high ranking Nazi officials to exterminate all 11,000,000 Jews on the European continent - a diabolical plan which was to become " *Hitler's Final Solution for the Jewish Problem in Europe* ". . And the effect of this 'change of heart' in post-war Germany with its emphasis on tolerance, especially towards Jews, and mutual respect at the primary and senior school levels, is also generally evident in industrial relations and throughout government organisations. In fact in all sections of public and political life, the German people have learnt to be more tolerant, and therefore more aware of the need for dialogue and compromise.

Training the young in the spirit of cooperation and respect, is Germany's ongoing assurance and moral commitment to her European Union partners and indeed to the world, that the frequently heard cry '*Nie Wieder !!*' (Never Again), is a sincere and genuine expression of the people's determination to learn from the past and to build a safer and better future for coming generations. The ongoing dialogue between Germans and Jews as symbolised by the Reconciliation Program, has therefore to be seen as an important milestone in this nation's moral transformation.

The Importance Of November 9th

T here is no greater proof of this public change of heart, than the huge demonstration on Nov. 9th 2000 at the Brandenburg Gate, when over 200,000 Berliners from all walks of life marched through the City to show their solidarity against racial intolerance and continuing worldwide abuse of human rights. And it is certainly no coincidence that this demonstration was timed for **Nov. 9th**, which in German history is both a day of national shame and also a symbol of national freedom and hope. The following four dates in German history are especially significant:

November 9th 1918 was the day on which the Weimar Republic was proclaimed from the Reichstag building. A large inscription above the entrance, dedicated by Kaiser Wilhelm II is a permanent reminder to all Germans that this attempt to democratize the German political system after WW I, was "FOR THE GERMAN PEOPLE".

November 9th 1923 was the infamous date of the so-called "*Munich Putsch*", when the newly formed DAP; the German Workers Party, under their leader Adolf Hitler failed in its attempt to topple the democratically elected Weimar government. Following his arrest, in one of the most dramatic court proceedings in German history, Hitler eloquently persuaded the judges that he was the only man capable of saving Germany from political anarchy. With a much reduced sentence, Hitler was taken to Landsberg Prison where he utilized the time to write 'Mein Kampf" (My Struggle), an exposé and manifesto of the National Socialist concept for a New World Order dominated by a *'purified German race'*. 'Mein Kampf' outlined Hitler's megalomaniac vision aimed at the worldwide extermination of all Jews, Negroid, Slavonic races and other politically 'undesirable elements'. For the Jewish people, this concept later became the 'blueprint' for what the Nazis called *"The Final Solution for the Jewish Problem in Europe"*. After Hitler's succession to power in 1933, the DAP became the NSDAP – the National Socialist German Workers Party, notorious for many acts of violence against opponents of the Nazi regime.

But for Jews who survived the infamous *'Reichskristallnacht'*, or (*The Night of Broken Glass*) of *November 9th 1938*, that date will for

29

ever be remembered for its unmitigated brutality against them and their property. For those Jews later unable to save themselves, that event became the prelude for their deportation to the death camps of Auschwitz and other extermination centres in the East.

The night of November 9th began with the nationwide burning of almost 200 Jewish synagogues and the destruction of over 7500 Jewish shops and cultural sites throughout Germany. But not only Nazi storm troopers, the SS (Black Shirts) and police were the perpetrators - in many instances, ordinary German citizens whipped up by Dr.Göbbels' (The Propaganda Minister) vicious anti-Semitic propaganda, saw in the *Reichskristallnacht* an opportunity to wreak their vengeance on the Jews – *'The Enemy In Their Midst.'* The need for Germans to 'save themselves' from the Jews who were, (according to Nazi propaganda), *'bent on destroying the German people'*, was the principal policy in a deliberate campaign to turn ordinary citizens against their Jewish neighbours. The arrest and nationwide deportation of more than 20,000 Jewish men to Dachau, Oranienburg, Sachsenhausen and other concentration camps which followed the November 9th pogrom, is generally regarded as the beginning of Hitler's campaign to exterminate all European Jews. The Nazis even invented a name to describe the objective for this mass extermination program. They planned to make first Germany, and then the whole of Europe, *'Judenrein'* i.e. 'Cleansed of all Jews'. To make every German City *'Judenrein'* became the official war cry which in 1941 unleashed Hitler's *"Final Solution For The Jewish Problem in Europe"*- and subsequently led to the systematic mass murder of almost 6,000,000 Jewish men, women and children.

But, with the breaching of the Berlin Wall. on ***November 9th 1989,*** this memorable date took on a much more positive meaning when it became the symbol of freedom and renewed hope for the German people. For it was on that date, after more than 44 years of Soviet occupation, when thousands of East Berliners streamed through the breached wall at the Brandenburger Gate, - heralding the freedom of the City which had been divided for so long. With Communist domination finally broken, the effect of Berlin's liberation was soon lauded worldwide and the determination of Berliners to be *'free'* has become the symbol of hope for many other organisations fighting for their own political independence. *(See Memorial Photo Page 57)*

The real importance of this event was however not even the actual breaching of the Berlin Wall - it was the message the German nation gave to the world. Never again would the German people tolerate any form of political dictatorship, whether it be from the extreme right as under the National Socialists, or from the extreme left as under the former Communist East German Republic. The *November 9th 2000* mass demonstration in Berlin and similar public protests in other German cities in support of personal freedom should therefore be seen not as isolated events, but as important milestones in the nation's progress on the difficult road towards becoming a mature democratic society.

In the German / European context, these public expressions for freedom are therefore part of an <u>ongoing</u> campaign against anything, which might threaten many years of hard-won democratic struggle for a united Germany. As Herr Eberhard Diepgen says: *"Such a moral crusade cannot be driven solely by legislation and State control - this is the challenge which both the State <u>and</u> the community must face together."*

Berliners from the former Soviet Zone of Occupation sitting on the Berlin Wall in defiance of East German border guards

THE BERLIN REICHSKRISTALLNACHT
NOVEMBER 9th 1938

Boycott And Destruction Of Jewish Shops

> # WARNING
> ## Jewish Shop
> ### All Customers Will Be Photographed

L - Jewish shops in the Berlin CBD earmarked for destruction on the Reichskristallnacht November 9th 1938. Nationwide, more than 7500 shops were destroyed and vandalized

R - *(Placard)*

> *"The Jewish proprietors of this 5 P.S. shop are pests and grave diggers of German craft. They only pay a 'hunger wage' to German workers. The proprietor is the Jew Nathan Schmidt"*

THE AFTERMATH OF THE BERLIN REICHSKRISTALLNACHT
NOVEMBER 9th 1938

Streets Littered With Glass And Jews Humiliated

L - Smashed glass from Jewish shops litter the streets of the Berlin Central Business District.

R - Elderly Jews are made to scrub Berlin streets for the amusement of the crowds.

Destruction Of Synagogues

L - The charred remains of a Jewish Synagogue with all its priceless treasures destroyed during the Reichskristallnacht of Nov. 9th

R - One of the many Synagogues set alight during the pogrom night. Fire fighters were prevented by S.A. Storm Troopers from extinguishing the flames

A group of neo-Nazis from the northern Italian city of Bolzano have travelled to the German concentration camp of Dachau where they posed for photos giving the Nazi salute.

Four members of the far-right German band Race War went on trial accused of forming a criminal organization that promoted racial hatred and glorified the Nazi era. The band also stands accused of using banned Nazi symbols. In 2003, prosecutors said, a "special edition" of its now-banned debut CD was issued on Adolf Hitler's birthday, with the Nazi dictator's picture and a swastika on the cover.

Beware Of The Danger From Within

U ndoubtedly, one of today's greatest political challenges for the Jewish communities in Germany (now numbering approximately 40,000), comes from Neo-Nazi groups who, just like in Hitler's day, regard the re-emerging influence of a growing Jewish cultural and commercial presence as a *"national threat to the German people from International Zionism"*. It is therefore naive to pretend that this danger from within does not exist and that the positive outlook referred to earlier, applies to the whole nation – ***of course it does not!*** In all democratic societies, there will always be dissenters – people who have genuine or imagined grievances against the government or specific organisations. Indeed, the ability and right to express one's political dissent in a non-violent way is at the very heart of the democratic principle. However, although in theory, it is the government's responsibility to guarantee a free press and the citizen's right to free speech, in reality, the concept of *'democracy'* is not an *'absolute'* but a *'relative'* term. Like other Communist totalitarian systems, such as the Peoples' Republics of China and North Korea, the former East German Democratic Republic, (DDR) also regarded itself as *'democratic'*. In reality however, as in any one-party State such as the Nazi regime and the Communist Soviet Union, East German citizens, lived in constant fear of denunciation and arrest and were regarded by those in power as little more than *'Property Of The State'*. In every aspect of their lives, as in the former Soviet Union, East Germans were the victims of a political system where any dissent was ruthlessly suppressed and neither freedom of speech nor a free press were tolerated.

In contrast, today's united Federal Republic of Germany represents all sides of the political spectrum in the Bundestag, the Lower House of Parliament and the Bundesrat, the Upper House. There are however, certain aspects relating to the political responsibilities of governments which have a special meaning in the German context and which strike at the very heart of their hard won democratic system. One of these, arising out of the nation's violent past, is the difficulty of setting 'acceptable' boundaries to control extreme political behaviour, especially that of Neo-

Nazi type organisations, whilst still guaranteeing to all citizens freedom of speech and a free press.

Is it better for society to accept a certain degree of violent behaviour by extreme right or left wing minority groups, and thereby uphold the spirit of *'democratic freedom'*, or should such conduct be controlled by State Legislation and the police? Should Federal parliament be empowered to make membership of Neo-Nazi organisations and fanatical religious groups illegal, and should the State have the right to confiscate vital material and financial assets of such organisations? To what extent should electronic surveillance systems such as private line tapping and spy cameras be used to prevent any political unrest and possible attack from terrorists? But again, would such government restrictions then not be seen as 'A *step too far'*, an unwarranted restriction of individual freedom, reminiscent of a 'Nazi style' suppression of democratic rights? Indeed, there is a very fine line between these two points of view.

These then are just some of the challenging and ongoing issues facing the German Parliament and the Berlin administration. It is therefore encouraging to recall Herr Diepgen's remarks, that the prevention of racial violence against Jews and other minorities is seen by the Senate as a high priority and to know that German authorities are actively working together with other European law enforcement agencies to combat the constant threat to society from extreme right and left wing organisations as well as fanatical religious groups.

One of the greatest problems is of course how to deal with the source of this evil in a modern democratic society. In this regard, the dissemination of increasingly aggressive material on Internet Web sites is now one of the most serious threats to law and order anywhere in the world. Unfortunately, even with the latest technology, the illusive nature of the Internet presents unique problems, in that site operators who entice viewers to violence against Jewish or other ethnic communities are difficult to trace on the Net and if found, even more difficult to prosecute.

But website violence is certainly not only a German problem - like malicious computer viruses, this pernicious evil, particularly with the increase in worldwide terrorist activities, threatens the stability of all societies worldwide. In Europe, however, this situation is made even more difficult by the disparity in the laws which govern the publishing and distribution of racially offensive material on the Web in different countries of the European Union. Although German Federal laws are in place to control acts of extreme civil disobedience and political violence, it is hardly surprising that the social and economic upheaval which accompanied the reunification of East and West Germany in the early 1990s, also saw increasing activity by Neo-Nazis and other radical groups. On the one hand, this destabilisation was made worse by the difference in living standards between the former socially unstable DDR with its legacy of more than 40 years of Soviet economic mismanagement, and on the other hand, the more affluent West with its strong American emphasis on capitalism and private enterprise. This social inequality provided a favourable climate for the expansion of radical non-conformist groups and dissidents. Two further factors did little to defuse the politically and economically volatile situation after reunification. The first was the severe demoralizing effect which the demise of the Communist DDR had on many older East Germans who, twice in a lifetime had seen their political utopia shattered and now found themselves in a *'political vacuum'*, highly sceptical and antagonistic towards any new social reform. The second has to do with the political organisation in Soviet East Germany where, as under Hitler, effective population control depended heavily on thousands of informers willing to denounce their neighbours to the authorities for financial gain. Some of these 'agents' had been well rewarded for their 'Services to the State' and had over the years profited handsomely from their lucrative treachery. With the collapse of the DDR, such personal enrichment and prestige came abruptly to an end. Now, deprived of their ill-gotten gains, and already skilled in covert STASI (German Secret Police) operations, such former betrayers soon found themselves attracted to newly emerging extremist groups and black marketeers operating in the now unified capital. Inevitably, before long, such organisations came in conflict with the police and city authorities.

The extent of this 'Big Brother' espionage net in the former DDR only became apparent after the collapse of the Communist system. Like the Soviet Union, to ensure all citizens accepted and maintained party loyalty, a vast army of secret police, state police and informers was required to deal with any citizen brave enough to defy the authorities or refuse to toe the 'official' Party line. To this end, the notorious STASI East German Secret Police, maintained a vast filing system of secret documents, tapes and files on every citizen which, according to some estimates, if placed end to end, would exceed 80 Kms. in length. There were also countless correspondence files and taped telephone conversations relating to West German government politicians and allied personnel which STASI officers had been unable to destroy when the collapse of the DDR became imminent. This immense database contained extremely sensitive and incriminating material, dealing with the most intimate details concerning Western leaders and officials. These highly classified documents were later to be presented as evidence of corruption in the trial of the dismissed CDU Chancellor Helmut Kohl, charged with impropriety and 'shady deals' relating to the sale of German tanks and other military hardware to Saudi Arabia to obtain party funds, (The so-called "CDU Spendenaffähre"). Fortunately, for the Chancellor, the courts finally decided against allowing any secret STASI material to be used as evidence against him and other CDU officials.

Wooden crosses at the former Checkpoint Charlie Border Crossing commemorate the many East German civilians who tried and failed to reach freedom during the time of the Soviet occupation.

THE FALL OF THE BERLIN WALL
NOVEMBER 9th 1989

The End Of 44 Years Of Soviet Domination

THE BRANDENBURGER TOR

This most famous of all Berlin landmarks has been at the centre of political strife ever since it was built in 1788. During the Nazi era, the Brandenburger Tor was the venue for many anti-Jewish demonstrations. During Soviet occupation, the Berlin Wall ran across the front of the building, splitting the City of Berlin into East and West. In 1962, US President J.F.Kennedy made his famous declaration "*Ich bin ein Berliner* " ("I am a Berliner") from a platform in front of the Brandenburger Tor.   On November 9th 1989, thousands of East Germans streamed through the breach of the Wall and to freedom in the West. This bid for freedom has been compared to the Exodus of the Jews from Egyptian slavery under their leader Moses and has become the symbol for freedom of all oppressed people worldwide. Today, demonstrations are mainly in support of democratic and human rights.

The Joy of Liberation
November 9th 1989

BERLIN IS AGAIN ONE UNITED CITY

THE FALL OF THE BERLIN WALL
NOVEMBER 9th 1989

Berliners Celebrate The Day Of Liberation

The end of the DDR. Liberated Berliners from East and West celebrate their newly won freedom on the "Wall Of Shame" where many died in their attempt to reach freedom in the West.

The Taste Of Freedom

Young Berliners celebrate reunion from the top of the Wall and the Brandenburger Gate

The Jewish Presence And The Berlin Senate

O ne of the strongest impressions during our visit to the capital was the City Administration's ongoing support for the Jewish communities, a welcome assurance for those Jews who were now visiting the capital for the first time since their pre-WW II expulsion. For all who once called this city their *'Heimat'* – their home, now brought together from every corner of the world by the Reconciliation Program, the Berlin experience is a forceful reminder of their past. Everything they now experience as senior citizens brings back memories of their childhood in the unending search for rational answers to questions which in fact may not even have answers, and are often too complex to define. Particularly, those guests who still harbour traumatic memories of their childhood need to find answers which will help them to understand not only the reality of the re-established Jewish presence in German society, but also as in pre-war days, the relevance of the growing Jewish influence on the commercial, artistic and political life of the nation. For ex-Berlin Jews it is particularly difficult to rationalize their own childhood experience during the Nazi period with today's official political tolerance in a democratic environment and the generally *'tolerant'* attitude of German society. But for all Jews with a German pre-war background who had first hand experience of Nazi brutality when they were young, the two most urgent questions must be:

1. *How effective is the current German political system to ensure the safety of Jews now resettled in Germany?*

2 *What legal measures are in place to curb Neo-Nazi activities directed against Jewish individuals and communities?*

Surprisingly, but perhaps in anticipation of 'official' answers to some of these questions by German and Jewish authorities, these concerns were only rarely, if at all, openly expressed by the visitors during our stay in the capital. Also, from brief discussions with a number of guests, it would seem that certain aspects regarding the Jewish question as explained by some Bundestag representatives were not always perceived by them as being based on a realistic understanding of their childhood experiences and were generally regarded as somewhat *'inadequate'*, and not very *'reassuring'*.

There is also another factor which influences the German/Jewish relationship at this time, for the current official supportive attitude towards Jewish communities has also to be seen against the background of the continuing inflow of foreign refugees into the Federal Republic from Africa, Asia and the Middle East. Opening the doors to this flood of suffering humanity has done little to alleviate the increasingly difficult social and economic situation facing the Berlin Senate since reunification.

Ever since the sudden demise of the DDR in November 1989, an enormously heavy financial burden has been placed on the Berlin City administration, which even 11 years after reunification (2000), is still smarting under the enforced investment of Millions of DM (Pre-Euro German currency) into the former Soviet zone, mainly because of the neglected infrastructure of the East German road and rail systems. This financial legacy is in part due to high interest repayments on borrowed capital by the City of Berlin which in the year 2000, we were told, were already millions of DM per day. Furthermore, added to the City's woes, many of the financial problems are very much related to the contrasting living standards between East and West and even in 2006, unemployment in the former Soviet Zone is still about twice as high as in the West with the total number of unemployed in the Federal Republic again exceeding five Million. So, looking at the German situation from an overall point of view, there is no doubt that much of the present high unemployment is still the legacy of years of neglect and mismanagement from the days of the DDR. Other factors, such as the unfavourable exchange rate of the Euro v. the $US, escalating oil prices and general problems facing the world economy, are of course also relevant factors.

As here in Australia, perhaps the most serious problem at this time (2006) to the German economy is the challenge presented by cheaper Asian labour markets, especially China, Taiwan and Korea. As an increasing number of German companies, attracted by low manufacturing costs relocate to Asia, this is having an marked effect on the German home labour market and as factories either 'restructure' or close down, large numbers of employees in the Federal Republic are retrenched, thus continuing the spiral towards mass unemployment. In the present situation, it is therefore not inappropriate to recall that when

Adolf Hitler took power in 1933, the unemployment situation was similar to what the country faces today and that it was in no small degree his ability to effectively solve this problem, which after 1933 gained him and the Nazi party much public support. That he achieved this 'economic miracle' by the establishment of a vast rearmament industry and the building of the Autobahn network, is history.It must surely be seen by all Jews as a clear indication of the administration's goodwill and changed German attitude not only towards returning Jews, but also towards ethnic minorities in general that, despite such major problems, the Berlin Senate continues to encourage Jewish immigration and strongly supports the already established Jewish communities in the capital.

Most importantly, Jewish cultural and commercial involvement *is again being accepted by the public as a 'normal' part of national life.* In this regard, like his predecessors, the former Mayor of Berlin, Herr Eberhard Diepgen, has clearly made a significant personal contribution to German/Jewish reconciliation. At a reception, following the official welcome of our group at the Berlin Town Hall, I was privileged to briefly speak with him in person. In answer to a question regarding the acceptance of Jewish integration by the public into German and particularly Berlin society, to my surprise, the Mayor responded with another question: *" Why do you ask me that "*? And then continued:

> *"In today's Germany, the question whether a person is Jewish or not, is no longer relevant."*

I was so impressed by this response that I decided to make this 'official' view the 'yard stick' (or should that be 'meter stick'?), whereby everything during the remainder of the Berlin visit could be 'assessed'.

As, day by day, the program unfolded, the conviction grew that these remarks were not merely born out of political expediency, but that despite enormous difficulties faced by the Senate, they actually represent a true picture of the official attitude towards the Jewish presence in the *NEW BERLIN* and that total Jewish integration into every aspect of city life is today no longer merely a ' target ', but an established reality. To see this changed attitude confirmed was for me one of the most important lessons to come out of the Berlin visit. Above all, I came to appreciate the administration's continuing difficulties in dealing with the spasmodic violent behaviour of various anti-Semitic groups in their midst and that the Program's success was to a large extent due to that administration's determination to exert the necessary political will to meet the challenges presented by the expanding Jewish and ethnic populations. After brief discussions with other officials, it became clear that in dealing with this difficult situation, the administration had not only shown unusual political courage in their willingness to face and learn from the realities of the past, but had by extensive dialogue with Jewish authorities also put into practice one of the basic principles of good management - by involving all parties affected by the decision making process.

Even after only one week, we were able to leave the capital, confident that under the present administration, the future of Jewish communities in Berlin was in good hands. The discrete presence of German police at all Jewish sites we visited provided further evidence that the present administration under the direction of the Governing Mayor, was more than capable of dealing with any Neo-Nazi threat which might arise against Jewish and other ethnic communities. It was especially important for me later to see confirmation of this in Herr Diepgen's own introduction to the booklet *"The Jewish Museum in Berlin"*, an informative publication presented to all guests at the end of their visit, where he affirms that:

> *"Jewish organisations are again playing an important role in the life of this challenging, ever changing, and exciting NEW BERLIN. Today, Jewish life has again taken its rightful place in the City and is once more shaping the face of the German capital ".*

Nothing, however, could give Jews, wherever they are, a greater assurance of Germany's continuing determination to make amends for the past, than the following excerpt from an article by the Mayor in the magazine *Aktuell* (64 / 1999 p.3).

> *"After WW II", he says ," We Germans made a solemn vow, never to forget the crimes of the past, to live up to our responsibilities and, as far as humanly possible, to make amends for the injustices for which we have been responsible. We have learned from each other and with each other to overcome the problems which divide us."*

These words are indeed reassuring for all Jews in Germany as well as those in the Diaspora that the already well established partnership between the Berlin Senate and the Jewish communities will continue and that the challenges of the 21st Century - whatever they might be - will be met.

PART III

The Berlin Tour
Reliving The Past
In The Present

Preparing For A Lifetime Experience

T he German / Jewish Reconciliation Program has to be seen not only as evidence of the nation's resolve to make amends for the past, but also in relation to the strong pre-war Jewish influence on German cultural, social and professional life. Indeed, when one considers that in 1933, the Jewish minority, comprising only *0.78 % of the total population,* occupied nearly 50% of all legal and professional positions in the capital Berlin, it is not difficult to see how this *'Alleged Zionist Threat To The German People'* became the perfect propaganda rationale for stirring up anti-Jewish feelings within the German population.* And so, with vicious anti-Semitic propaganda and unbridled brutality, in January 1942, Hitler's *'Final Solution'* – the plan to systematically destroy the Jewish presence in Europe, was set in motion. It is therefore indeed remarkable that this reconciliation program not only recognises the important role played by Jews in the past, but that by encouraging personal contact between former Jewish residents and German families, it becomes indirectly associated with the re-establishment of the once prominent Jewish commercial and academic influence in the life of the nation.

Because Jews who were forced out of Germany after 1936, had been progressively deprived by the Nazi government of almost all their assets and money, many who had settled in adopted countries, would normally have been unable to finance the expensive hotel and flight costs associated with the program. It is a measure of the organisers' goodwill that the Program not only covers all airfares to and from Berlin, but also provides for a week's accommodation in one of the City's best four star hotels. In addition, there is a generous allowance for shopping and personal needs.

Note: * *Similar conditions also applied on the industrial front. In the scrap metal industry for instance, all three dominant pre-war companies were under Jewish ownership and between them they controlled 90% of the entire German scrap metal market. – a major component in Nazi armament production.-.*

(Petra Bonavita (Hg) Assimilation,Verfolgung,Exil P30; Schmetterling Verlag)

Such an open-handed gesture for 34,000 participants over more than 30 years has to be seen as further evidence not only of the Senate's, but also of the peoples' change of heart in re-establishing German/Jewish friendship. To enable guests to make personal arrangements, prior to the visit, comprehensive literature and schedule details including a list of the group participants and information on Berlin's Jewish organisations, cemeteries, synagogues and other places of interest had been provided by the organisers. Such information was greatly appreciated by guests wishing to visit friends, relatives, or places which to them were of special importance.

Regrettably, because the Berlin visit was limited to only one week, it was not possible to provide more than a superficial overview of the City's rich historical, political, and cultural history, making the proceedings of necessity very time constrained. For reasons previously outlined in Part I, the Jewish guests came from every corner of the globe and the chance to recuperate in a luxurious hotel after their long flight, was a most welcome relief. Also, for me to share this experience with my only sister and her husband from England, added a very special dimension to the visit.

The program began with a City bus tour, a fitting introduction to the eventful week which lay ahead. But for these elderly Jewish guests who still remembered their childhood expulsion from this city, being back in Berlin meant much more than a mere ' *Sight Seeing Tour On A Bus'*. *For them,* it was *" A 'Personal' Wakeup Call to come to terms with their own traumatic past'* .

Somehow, at this point of the Berlin experience, the distinction between that past and the present reality of again being in the city where it all happened, seemed to merge into one indefinable time zone. It was, in a sense, like '*looking through the window of time'*, and as once familiar landmarks brought back distressing memories of childhood years, the uncertainty which all ex-German Jews have for their future, could already be seen in the faces of the guests.

Throughout the program, our two principal tour guides were Herr Reimar Volker, a most pleasant young man who had studied in England and Frau Hannelore Fobo. Both were fully bilingual in English and German and showed an impressive knowledge of Berlin's historic past. It was thanks to their sensitive handling of the Jewish memorial sites, that at least to some extent, this emotional experience became less traumatic

THE PROGRAM SCHDULE

T he program schedule shown below covers five separate aspects, two being allocated to each day, except for the City tour on day 1. For the sake of clarity however, each aspect is here dealt with separately. What follows, is a summary of the impressions gained and lessons learnt from these daily activities.

    a)   **City Tours**

    b)   **Visit to Jewish sites**

    c)   **Official Contacts**

    d)   **Entertainment**

    e)   **Personal Free Time**

<u>Note</u>: *A list of illustrations for items marked in* ***Bold Italic*** *is given on Pages ix & x in the Preliminaries Section.*

(a) *The Berlin City Tour*

Berlin is a fascinating city with a conflicting past stretching back over 760 years. Since our emigration in 1939, I had been back only once on a lightning one day visit in 1993 and the changes which had taken place since then in the Central Business District, were immediately apparent. Especially noticeable were the large building sites near the Reichstag and the Potsdamer Platz. My initial impression was of a well planned city environment with large open squares and wide tree lined avenues, architectural features reminiscent of pre-war Berlin. There is so much to see in the German capital, that even a slow bus tour cannot do full justice to the great changes that have taken place since reunification.

Viewed from a touring bus, it is difficult to fully grasp the historical significance of the city's famous landmarks, as one by one, they glide slowly *'like ships in the night'* past the window. For Jews, who lived here in pre-war times, many of these monuments recalling Germany's military past, bring back painful memories of the Nazi era. As each in turn faded from view, I felt that such reminders of Germany's past military glory were somehow 'out of keeping' in a country striving towards European unity and peaceful co-existence, especially with her former enemy France. What memories of their childhood days, I wondered, would this tour bring back for the Jewish guests, and in a wider sense, what message do some of these landmarks give not only to them, but also to future German generations? How for instance, can one on the one hand, reconcile the decision to leave the almost totally destroyed *Kaiser Friedrich Wilhelm Memorial Church* in its ruined state as a permanent reminder to the German people of the futility of war, and on the other hand, restore to its former glory the severely damaged 67 Mtr. high *Siegessäule Victory Column.* This prominent Berlin landmark with its golden Goddess of Victory and 'girdle' of captured French canons, not only commemorates Prussian victories over France, Austria and Denmark, but also permanently reminds Berliners of the unification of German states under Otto von Bismarck in 1871. As the bus drove past, I could not help wondering why, contrary to the present emphasis on 'peaceful coexistence' with Germany's former enemies, this memorial to past Prussian militarism had been restored to its former prominence.

No matter where one goes in Berlin, there is a reminder of Germany's historic and military past. The burnt out remains of the *Kaiser Friedrich Wilhelm Memorial Church, The Schöneberg Town Hall,* from where thousands of Jews and others deemed 'undesirable' by the Nazi authorities were subjected to a mock trial before being sent to the death camps, the *Berlin Cathedral,* last resting place of the Hohenzollern dynasty, '*Checkpoint Charlie',* the former control point between the American and Soviet occupation zones and the *Brandenburger Tor,* focal point of many Nazi rallies, are just some of the City's many historical landmarks which in the past, not only shaped and influenced the history of Berlin and the German nation, but in two World Wars also determined the destiny of Europe and the world.

Older readers will recall that it was from a platform overlooking the Soviet sector in front of the *Brandenburger Tor,* where in 1962 the late US President J.F.Kennedy made his famous declaration: "*Ich bin ein Berliner"!,* ("I am a Berliner"). During the Nazi era, the Brandenburger Tor was the scene of many political demonstrations. It was here, that the infamous Berlin Wall first began to crumble in November 1989 and thousands of East Berliners streamed through the gates into the Western sector of the city, heralding the birth of the *NEW BERLIN*, capital of a *UNITED* Federal Republic of Germany.

Although, many new buildings are under construction in the Central Business District, nowhere is this building activity more apparent than at the *Potsdamer Platz*, Europe's largest construction site, where overhead cranes tower high above what was once a barren waste land – legacy of long time Soviet occupation. (*See Photo Page53*).Another huge construction site is in the vicinity of the *Reichstag* Building where the Future Federal Government Administrative Offices are slowly taking shape. Extensive building activity is also evident at the *Pariser Platz* near the *Brandenburger Tor*, as well as in many Western suburbs of the City.

Wherever possible, as a reminder of Berlin's historic past, prominent old buildings like the *Schloss Bellevue*, built in 1785 for Prince August Ferdinand, youngest son of Frederick the Great, are being restored to their former state. This fine building was almost totally destroyed by allied bombing during the war, but has now been fully restored as the German president's residence.

As part of the reconstruction program near the Brandenburger Tor, 55 years after the liberation of the concentration camps, and after almost 12 years of contention over the most suitable design, the construction of a memorial to the 6,000,000 murdered Jewish victims of the Nazi Holocaust is to commence in 2001* Another interesting landmark is the East-West *Memorial in the Tauentzienstrasse*, one of the main central avenues in the City. Wherever one looks, Berlin is truly a City of Memorials – a constant reminder of its tumultuous past.

Berliners are also very proud of the City's '*green belts*', parks and gardens and a particularly pleasing aspect of the *NEW BERLIN* is the harmonious blending of green areas with new building work. Of all the public parks, the *Tiergarten*, (literally 'Animal Garden') in the City centre is one the most popular. Today, this beautiful park which was once the Elector's private hunting ground, is again the City's pride and joy. At the end of the war, Berlin citizens, desperately short of fuel, were forced to fell all the trees in the park for firewood and it took many years of replanting to restore the park to its former self.

In its role as the cultural centre of Europe, Berlin has always been famous for its museums. Most of these are situated on an island of the river Spree appropriately named "*The Museuminsel*"(The Museum Island).

THE KAISER FRIEDRICH WILHELM MEMORIAL CHURCH

T he rare pre-war photo below (L), is the original church built by Kaiser Wilhelm II between 1891–1895 as a memorial to his grandfather Frederick. Photo (R) shows the ruins of the church after it was badly damaged in WW II air raids. After the war, the decision was made not to level the site but to leave what remained of this famous building in its ruined state, as a permanent reminder of the futility of war.

Pre-War photo of the Memorial Church   Photo taken in 2000

View from the Kurfürstendamm

52

REBUILDING THE CITY OF BERLIN
THE POTSDAMER PLATZ

I n pre-war days, this huge square at the centre of the Berlin CBD was one of the busiest in Europe. In 1961, the Soviets bulldozed the entire area behind the Berlin Wall and created a huge ' No Mans Land ' at the centre of the City. The photo below left shows the barren wasteland, where during the Soviet occupation, 24 hour armed police supervision on watch towers ensured that any attempt at escape by East Berliners, was doomed to failure. After reunification, a massive rebuilding program of offices, theatres and commercial enterprises was initiated, employing some of the world's most prominent architects. The pictures below show the dramatic transformation of the area since the fall of the Berlin Wall in November 1989 with new shopping centres and commercial buildings.

From Soviet Wasteland

To Berlin's Culture And Business Centre

THE SIEGESSÄULE

This famous Victory Column in the Tiergarten was erected in 1873 to commemorate Prussian victories over France, Austria and Denmark and the declaration of the 1st German Reich under Otto von Bismarck in 1871. The vertical columns are French canons captured in various military campaigns. An internal staircase leads to a platform at the top with a magnificent view of the City. The monument was rebuilt after being badly damaged by Russian shelling in WW II.

THE BRANDENBURGER TOR

For more than forty years, the lifeless square in front of the Brandenburger Tor marked the demarcation between the Soviet and American sectors of occupation in the centre of the City. The Berlin Wall, erected in 1961, ran along the front of the gate and unauthorised entry to either the East or West was virtually impossible. A nearby memorial plaque commemorates those who were shot by East German guards attempting to cross to the West through the Berlin Wall. Today, the large square in front of the Brandenburger Tor, known as Pariser Platz, is the site of various foreign embassies.

THE REICHSTAG BUILDING

The Reichstag after WW II destroyed in 1945 by the Red Army

A fter Kaiser Wilhelm II laid the foundation stone in 1882, construction continued between 1884 and 1894. Under the Weimar Republic, (2nd. Reich), the building was used by the German Parliament. In 1935, a disastrous fire (falsely blamed on Communists and Jews), destroyed most of the building, and the Reichstag was never fully rebuilt during the Nazi era. In 1945, the massive building was almost totally destroyed by Russian shelling.

The Reichstag Building
without the dome

The Reichstag Building
with the restored dome

R econstruction of the Reichstag building after WW II was completed in 1970 but did not include the original glass dome. Before the reestablishment of the Federal Parliament in Bonn / Rhein, part of the building with its large assembly hall and conference rooms was used by both German Houses of Parliament. In 1999, the Reichstag Building was finally completed with the cupola dome, after a British architect, Sir Norman Foster had made extensive alterations and had redesigned the interior. In September 2000, the new Reichstag was officially inaugurated with full public access. Both Houses of Parliament, (The Bundestag and the Bundesrat) are now reinstalled in their respective assemblies.

THE SCHÖNEBERG TOWN HALL

B uilt in 1911, this famous Town Hall has a long and varied history. Before the war, it was the Supreme Court of Justice but during WW II, the Town Hall was taken over by the infamous 'People's Court' where 'justice' was solely based on Nazi racial ideology. During WW II, thousands of Jews and other 'Enemies Of The People' were sentenced to imprisonment and death from here. After the war, the building was used by the Allied Control Council. From 1948 till reunion in 1989, the Town Hall was the seat of the Berlin Senate. In 1954, the Four Power Conference convened here and in 1971 the Four Power Berlin Agreement was concluded in this building. Today, (2000), it houses the Four Power Allied Air Security Centre.

THE SCHLOSS BELLEVUE

T his beautiful building, near the Tiergarten, was originally built for Prince August Ferdinand, the youngest son of Frederick the Great. Schloss Bellevue, almost completely destroyed by allied bombing during WW II, was fully restored, and since 1959 has been the official residence of the President of the Federal Republic of Germany.

THE TAUENTZIENSTRASSE MEMORIAL

A view from the Tauentzienstrasse, one of the city's main boulevards looking in the direction of the ruined Kaiser Friedrich Wilhelm Memorial Church. The small building (arrowed), just to the left of the tower, is a memorial shrine made up of thousands of glass fragments collected during reconstruction from the bombed-out church. The impressive Berlin memorial in the foreground was erected during the Soviet occupation of East Berlin. It symbolises a city physically divided yet united by a common bond – the yearning for freedom.

THE TIERGARTEN WITH THE VICTORY MEMORIAL

The magnificent Tiergarten, once the Elector's private hunting ground, with the Victory Memorial at the centre. During the war, and the bitter winters of the post war period, all the trees were felled for firewood. After several years of intense replanting, the Tiergarten is once again the delight of all Berliners. The long avenue is the Bismarckstrasse which goes through to the Brandenburger Gate, seen at the end of the green belt, and then becomes the famous 'Unter Den Linden' avenue.

THE BERLIN PERGAMON MUSEUM

O f particular interest is the **Pergamon Museum,** ranking among the world's greatest Archaeological Exhibition Centres with its magnificent restored **Ishtar Gate** and the world famous **Pergamon Altar** from which the museum derives its name. Until the German archaeologist Robert Koldewey discovered the ruins of the City of Babylon in 1887 in what is now Southern Iraq, only a small placard on the Baghdad railway line inscribed *'Babylon Halt'* reminded the traveller of the great Babylonian empire which once ruled the world. During the Soviet occupation, the Ishtar Gate and other exhibits were taken to Russia, but were later returned to the Pergamon Museum. The beautiful *Pergamon Altar* excavated at Bergama in Turkey and dating back to 180-160 BC with its pure white marble displayed under a sunlit glass roof is a magnificent sight. In 1938, the Nazis closed this museum as well as all other places of national culture to Jews.

The Berlin Pergamon Museum situated on the Museum Island

The Pergamon Museum also holds some very personal memories because it was solely due to the following chance event, that we were able to visit these two exhibits on the very last day, before the doors were shut. It was in 1938 - my mother was reading the paper, when she suddenly jumped up, and seized my sister and myself by the arm. Hurrying down the stairs and through the busy streets of Berlin, she explained breathlessly that under a new decree, Nazi authorities were about to ban Jews from all cultural centres and, if we survived, this was the last day on which it would be possible for us to see the Ishtar Gate and the white marble Pergamon Altar at the Museum before we left Germany. *And she was right!* The next day, all Jews were banned, not only from museums, but also from concert halls, art galleries, sporting facilities and all other venues of cultural interest.

Of all the humiliation the Nazi decrees imposed on German Jews, this was one of the most devastating. Despite the escalating persecution, many Jews, especially those who had fought for Germany during WW I, never forgot their German heritage, often going back Centuries. Even many of the strictly orthodox considered themselves more 'German' than 'Jewish'. This reluctance to face the inevitable truth about the Nazi persecution and the serious situation that was now facing them, became an important factor for those who were later unable to leave the country. Having been nurtured from childhood in the belief that all music and forms of artistic expression were sacrosanct, especially middle class Jews were very conscious of traditional German art and music. In a very real sense, they regarded all national culture as part of that rich German artistic heritage to be enjoyed by all, regardless of race or religion. Suddenly to be deprived of what they considered to be 'their cultural right', and the thought of no longer being able to attend Mozart or Beethoven concerts, to say nothing of already banned composers like Mahler, Mendelssohn, or world famous soloists like Yehudi Menuhin, Jascha Heifetz and Arthur Rubinstein etc. and to be denied the right to visit famous Art galleries and to hear the great Italian operas, was for many Jews a humiliation almost too hard to bear.

THE BERLIN PERGAMON MUSEUM

The Ishtar Gate with its mythological animal figures embossed on a blue glazed background was once the main exit from the Processional Avenue to the City of Babylon. As shown below, it was originally brought to the museum in the form of thousands of excavated fragments which had to be sorted and placed in the exact position they once occupied 2500 years ago. Seeing the Ishtar Gate and other exhibits such as the Pergamon Altar from ancient Turkey for the first time is an unforgettable experience for the thousands of visitors who visit the museum each year.

The Ishtar Gate
Exit to the City Of Babylon Processional Way

L -The world's biggest jigsaw puzzle! Thousands of excavated fragments from The Processional Way being sorted and itemised.

R -The white marble Pergamon Altar, dating back to the 2nd Century BC and dedicated to the Greek patron goddess Athena.

Reminiscences Of A Childhood Past

A s the touring bus slowly made its way down the famous Unter den Linden avenue (Under The Lime Trees) and along the Kurfürstendamm, many personal memories of the past came flooding back. More than anything, I remembered the apartment at ***No. 160 Kurfürstendamm,*** where we lived until our emigration to England in March 1939. At the front entrance to No. 160 sat the so-called 'Blockwart', an official 'flat supervisor' who recorded details of every occupant (especially Jews) name of visitors and the flat visited, purpose of the visit, time of arrival, and estimated time of departure. On leaving, the stated and actual times of departure were compared and any discrepancies recorded. This information was then passed to the Gestapo (Secret Police), a provision which later greatly facilitated the identification and location of Jewish families for arrest and deportation.

The author and his sister outside No.160 Kurfürstendamm, now a retirement home for the elderly. The white dot marks our living room.

One of the highlights of the Berlin visit therefore had to be No.160 Kurfürstendamm. After some explanations to the receptionist lady at the front desk regarding the purpose of our visit, she kindly escorted us to our old apartment on the third floor. Surprisingly, despite extensive alterations, we could still recognize our former home and much looked like it was when we left in 1939. Like most former Jewish homes, during the war, No. 160 was taken over by an unknown German family after their own home had been destroyed by Allied bombing. It would have been most interesting to meet these people. The house is now a retirement home for wealthy clients, with its own attached restaurant, private sauna, and 24 hour medical supervision.

As the bus continued on its tour, I remembered the Swastika flags at every window all down the Kurfürstendamm and the large banners at street intersection proclaiming to Berliners that *"The Jews Are Our Misfortune"*. It was mandatory for all German citizens, except Jews to display such flags and non-compliance was classified by the Nazis as *'An Act Of Defiance Against The State'*, subject to severe penalties. I remember the Jewish shops along the Kurfürstendamm earmarked with the Star of David in readiness for their intended destruction on November 9th 1938, the infamous Reichs-kristallnacht. Outside every Jewish shop a placard warned Germans that if they entered, they would be photographed. (*See Page 32*). And, especially, I remember how, as a 12 year old, when it was dangerous for Jewish children to be seen alone in the streets, I watched through our 3rd floor curtains, S.A. Storm troopers marching down the Kurfürstendamm singing:

> "Wir sind die Herren der Welt
> Wir tun was uns gefällt
> Heute gehört uns Deutschland
> Morgen gehört uns die Welt "

> *"We Are The Masters Of The World*
> *We Can Do Just As We Like,*
> *Today, Germany Is Ours,*
> *Tomorrow The World."*

And who can ever forget the terrible events on November 9th 1938, when mountains of glass, together with the contents of smashed Jewish shops, were strewn across the pavements of every German city? I vividly recall how our school bus had to be diverted that day because of the destruction and how, when we returned home at night, a large Jewish synagogue was still burning because S.A Storm Troopers had prevented the fire fighting services from extinguishing the flames. (*See Page 33*). I can also remember, when walking home from the bus stop that evening, seeing the S.A. dragging the owners of a shop out onto the street and the crowd shouting abuse at the elderly Jewish couple, whilst the shop contents were being loaded onto a truck. All this, and much more, came back into my consciousness, when in September 2000 the bus made its way down the Kurfürstendamm -Berlin's most famous avenue.

But most of all, I remembered the day in March 1939, when clutching a small suitcase and my precious violin, (now over 100 years old), my mother, sister and I left No.160 and made our way to the Anhalter Bahnhof railway station *, there to join hundreds of other Jewish children on the Kindertransport to England. Incredibly, even after more than 60 years and many house moves in England and Australia, I still have that same violin, (not, I have to confess, played too often these days). I even still have the original ship boarding pass for the nightmare passage from Hook Van Holland to Harwich on March 15th 1939, the worst crossing experienced by the ship's crew in more than 10 years.

Not until years later, did I fully appreciate the terrible dilemma which most Jewish children faced that day as they waited at the station for the train to take them out of Germany and an uncertain future. There were many heart wrenching scenes that day as parents said their final good byes and watched their children boarding the train for England. How many of those children, some only three and four years old, standing on that platform anxiously clutching their most precious toys and possessions, realised that this was to be the last time they would see their parents alive. Not until the end of the war would many of these youngsters, now in their teens, become aware that their parents had perished in one of the Nazi death camps.

Note: * *During the years of the Holocaust, the Anhalter Bahnhof became one of the major departure points for Jews destined for the extermination camps in the East.*

But, what about our own family ? How did we manage to get out ? After my father died, in addition to the constant harassment by Nazi authorities and fear of the future which made life increasingly uncertain for all Jews, my mother was left on her own to care for two children. However, compared with other Jewish families in Germany at that time, we were very fortunate indeed, for none of my family perished in the Holocaust, although my aunt fled to Prague just three days before the Germans marched into that city, and it is most unlikely that she would have survived her internment in Theresienstadt concentration camp. But most importantly, by the Grace of God, and due to circumstances which can only be described as 'miraculous', my mother who at 51 was already over the official Jewish emigration age limit, escaped arrest and thanks to the untiring efforts of certain individuals in England and my aunt in Berlin, was able to join us in England two months after our departure from Germany.

As for my sister and humble self, we were also saved by an extraordinary set of circumstances. It was in August 1938, when Jewish parents were frantically exploring every avenue of escape to save their children. In this hour of need, my mother remembered that as a 16 year old student, her parents had sent her to a prestigious private school in England, where she had befriended a girl, who was in fact the granddaughter of the famous 19th Century British scientist and writer Sir Thomas Huxley. Also, this girl's cousins, Aldous and Julian Huxley, attended the same school. Aldous later became a famous writer and is perhaps best remembered for his futuristic vision in 'Brave New World'. Sir Julian studied Botany, became Professor of Zoology, Kings College, London and held many eminent positions in Science, before being appointed Director General of UNESCO from 1946-48.

After both my mother and her friend had married and had their own families, correspondence between the two women gradually ceased and over the next 30 years they progressively lost touch with each other. But, as the situation for Jews in Germany was becoming more desperate by the day, the burning question now was: *"Would it be possible to locate this friend after all these years, and would she be willing and able to save the children?"* Miracles of miracles! It was eventually through the efforts of a distant English relative, that the two former school friends were brought together again. When my mother wrote and explained the desperate plight of the family in Berlin, her former school friend and husband, a retired Brigadier General in the British Army, immediately offered to act as guarantors for both my sister and myself until our 18th birthday, two years longer than was legally required. And so, through the Kindertransport organisation, and the unbounded generosity of these people, we became the guardian children of my mother's former school friend and her British Army general husband, the culmination of a saga which began in 1904, when my grandparents sent their 16 year old daughter to an English private school. Little did they know that this decision would, thirty four years later, be instrumental in saving their grandchildren from the Nazi terror and almost certain death. We are for ever grateful for the excellent schooling these wonderful people gave us, their loving care for so many years, and the many happy times we spent on their beautiful farm in Kent. My sister still keeps in touch with the daughter and her grown family in London.

Also, thanks to the determined efforts of my German Aunt, an English relative and certain other people in England, my uncle Walter, a former High Court Judge (until deposed by the Nazis), managed to escape to England, whilst his 'non-Jewish' wife, also a highly qualified legal professional, endured most of the terrible allied bombing which virtually destroyed the capital Berlin. It is indeed ironic that like so many other German/Jewish refugees who had fled to England, after being hounded in Germany by the Gestapo *for being Jewish*, my uncle was shortly after his arrival, interned by the British on the Isle of Man - *because he was German*. After spending the war in England, immediately after the cessation of hostilities in Europe, he was reinstated by US authorities as *Senatspräsident des Oberlandesgerichts Frankfurt/Main,* one of the highest German judiciary appointments during the early post-war period. He died in 1956. Another of my uncles, a dental surgeon, emigrated to New York and lived there with his family for many years until his death.

The sequel to this situation is also interesting, because it highlights the power of British democracy, and the effectiveness of what today is known as *'People Power'.* Despite wartime restrictions, after only six weeks, the arbitrary arrest and order for internment of foreign persons classified as 'enemy aliens', was quashed by Parliament because of the British public's outrage that the legal requirements pertaining to the so-called **HABEAS CORPUS ACT**, had not been complied with. This important act , which is still valid today, (except in a state of national emergency) makes it illegal for an agent of the crown to hold a prisoner for more than 24 hours without laying a specific charge against the accused. The act is part of a document known as **'The Magna Carta'**, originally signed by King John of England in **1216**. *(See next Page)*. The Charter severely restricted the king's power over the barons, and eventually laid the foundation for the British democratic Parliamentary System. Clearly, in the case of the arbitrary detainment of these men, whose only 'crime' was that they were Jewish refugees from Germany and other threatened countries, the **HABEAS CORPUS ACT'** had not been complied with and so, following a massive public protest, most internees were released.

And this already bizarre situation also had another twist, because by international law, most refugees were in fact not even *'German'* but *'stateless'* due to the Nazi decree which had deprived all Jews of their German citizenship before leaving the country.

Copy of the original *Magna Carta** document, dating back to the year 1216. Because the British government did not comply with the **HABEAS CORPUS CLAUSE** incorporated in this document during WW II, thousands of Jewish refugees held in custody on the Isle of Man had to be released.

Note:* *One of the original Magna Carta documents is held in the British Museum Library, London.*

The Aftermath Of The Reichskristallnacht For Jews -Arrests and Deportation

As mentioned previously, in many ways, my own family was exceptionally fortunate to survive these difficult times. Though sadly, my father had died from cardiac arrest two months before the November 9th Reichskristallnacht, in a way it was really a blessing in disguise. Suffering from a severe heart condition, he would never have survived deportation, let alone a prolonged stay at the notorious Oranienburg or Sachsenhausen concentration camps, where most Berlin Jews were taken following their arrest after the pogrom night. The stark reality of what was happening in these camps was brought home to me as a 12 year old boy by the following incident:

Our rented accommodation at No.160 Kurfürstendamm was part of a larger apartment occupied by a Jewish Lawyer Dr.Rippner and his wife. Whilst eating their evening meal on November 10th, the day after the Reichskristallnacht, there was a powerful knock on the door of the apartment, a sound which for all Jews at that time was like a 'death knell', heralding possible arrest by the Gestapo. *(See 'The Koppenplatz Memorial Page 104)*. Frau Dr.Rippner, a bundle of nerves, chronically obese and severely diabetic, slowly opened the door to be confronted by two fierce looking SS officers in black uniform demanding that " *Herr Dr.Rippner was to come immediately to the police station for interrogation* ". This was about the last thing this poor woman wanted to hear! The SS men stood impatiently at the apartment entrance and were totally unmoved by her anxiety, whilst my mother tried her best to usher us children into the living room, away from the scene which was about to unfold. *"Dr.Rippner"*, barked the SS man, *"had just 10 minutes to get ready and was to take only a small suitcase."* These were the days, when Jews could be arrested for the most trivial offences, like crossing the street at the wrong time or even 'looking suspicious'. What terrible crime then had Dr.Rippner committed to warrant this sudden arrest by the SS? The pronouncement that: *"It was only for interrogation and he would be back in a few days"*, did little to calm the distraught woman's fears and after a tearful 'good bye', Dr. Rippner in overcoat and hat and clutching his small suitcase, was arrested and taken away by the SS men. My mother tried to do what she could to restore some form of normality. Little did we or any other Jewish family know at that time that similar scenes were being enacted in countless other Jewish homes all over Germany. Even, after years of constant harassment and severe persecution by the Nazi authorities, it was difficult to comprehend, that these were not spontaneous arrests as in the past aimed at individuals, but rather the beginning of a nationwide, highly organised and deliberate campaign aimed at the destruction of the entire Jewish presence in Germany - to make the country '*Judenrein*', that is '*cleansed of all Jews.*' In fact, for those elderly Jews who would later be deported for extermination at Auschwitz or some other 'final destination' in the East, the organised violence against the Jewish communities which followed the night of November 9th 1938, heralded the true and ultimate intentions of the Nazi government.

For all German Jews, much worse was to come! Before long, their communities had to accept the awful truth that the arbitrary arrest of their menfolk was not in fact directed against individuals, but that the sole reason for this mass action was simply *because they were Jews*. Slowly, the awful truth was beginning to sink in - because from now on - **_no Jew was safe_** ; *Anyone* could face arrest and deportation at any time, any place. To add to Jewish woes, a new Nazi decree forced all males to identify themselves by the addition of the name '*Israel*'on all their documents, whilst the name '*Sarah*' became mandatory for all female Jews. This again facilitated identification and later arrest by the SS or Gestapo. Three years later, in 1941, the Nazis issued another decree making it mandatory for all Jews from the age of 16 to wear the yellow Star of David. This '*Mark of the Jew*' which had not been seen in Germany since the Middle Ages, greatly facilitated later arbitrary mass arrests and deportation. Non-compliance with all decrees carried extremely heavy penalties.

In the exceptionally severe winter of 1938, the plight of the arrested men now became even more serious because they had only been allowed to take with them a small suitcase, perhaps containing no more than a set of pyjamas and some toiletries. Without warm clothing to protect them against the extreme cold in the camps, the situation for the arrested men was rapidly becoming more critical by the day. As the news of the overnight nationwide disappearance of more than 20,000 Jewish men spread through the Jewish communities, a massive rescue operation organized by family members and volunteers went into action. But in reality, little could be done, because nobody knew where the arrested men were actually being held. In the absence of news from official Nazi sources, and the fear of reprisal against those who did know, it was just as if 20,000 men had simply *'vanished'* overnight, without a trace. As the hours turned to days and the days to weeks without a word from the authorities or the arrested men, there was near panic in many Jewish homes. But gradually, as the weeks went by, the news began to trickle through on the Jewish grapevine that most men from Berlin and the surrounding districts had been taken to one of the notorious concentration camps at Oranienburg or Sachsenhausen, East of the City. Immediately, the Jewish rescue organizations dispatched parcels with warm clothing, hoping that at least in this way, they could help their menfolk. But, even this act of compassion was to come to nought.

Is it possible to convey at this time to you the reader, the sheer terror these Jewish families must have experienced, when a few days later, all their parcels were returned with a large stamp: *"It is forbidden for prisoners of the Reich to receive any mail, including parcels!"*, and no indication as to how long their menfolk might still be imprisoned? Was it to be weeks, months, or even years? In fact, it was to be at least another six weeks of anxious waiting and hoping, before the men were released, after being made to sign a declaration, ensuring their 'silence'.

But eventually, they did come home, including Dr.Rippner. I remember clearly our mother trying to prevent my sister and myself from witnessing his return. What we did see, was a middle aged man, once full of energy and vitality, now looking like a living skeleton, being welcomed back by his panic stricken wife, after six weeks in Nazi custody. And the awful reality was that similar scenes were being enacted at this time in thousands of other Jewish homes in Berlin and throughout Germany as the menfolk returned from the Concentration Camps.

Following these events, most Jews could see that this was the beginning of the end, and there was now a frantic rush to complete the complicated formalities necessary for emigration. Whilst some succeeded in leaving Germany in time, either legally or illegally, many could not meet the stringent age requirements which had been set by Jewish relief organisations and were later deported to Auschwitz or other 'destinations in the East', where most Berlin Jews eventually perished.

And when in September 2000, the bus again passed No: 160 Kurfürstendamm, and the reality of the present merged strangely with the experiences of the past, I could not help thinking of Dr Rippner and his panic stricken wife and relive what happened in this place 62 years ago on that fateful evening of November 10th 1938. I believe, one of their sons managed to escape to Norway but, sadly after our own departure, we lost all trace of the family.

"Jewish Pig" - Graffiti sign marking Jewish shop in
Berlin's Central Business District

Aftermath Of The Reichskristallnacht
For the Nazi Government-A Massive Damage Bill

T he terrible events which occurred during the actual Reichskristallnacht, November 9th 1938, have already been highlighted earlier. In that one night, altogether more than 7500 Jewish shops, 191 Synagogues, 21 warehouses, 171 Jewish homes, and 11 Jewish community centres were vandalised and burnt,. an unprecedented orgy of destruction organised and executed by a government. In fact, it was the sudden, simultaneous burning of so many shops and especially the damage to large department stores, like Wertheim and the KDW in the Berlin CBD, which in the aftermath of the pogrom inadvertently became 'The Thorn In The Flesh' for the Nazi government who, in their frenzied hatred of the Jews, had given little consideration to the eventual consequences of their actions. As we shall see, this lack of foresight would soon have serious financial implications for the Nazis as well as the Jewish communities.

In preparation for the planned action on November 9th, Nazi authorities had earmarked all Jewish premises for destruction by painting a 'Star Of David' or some other offensive graffiti on front shop windows, in the belief that such shops were actually owned by Jewish proprietors. (*See Page 32*). This proved to be a fatal mistake! It was not until S.A. Storm Troopers, the SS, and thousands of ordinary citizens, whipped up by vicious anti-Jewish propaganda, had reaped their vengeance on what they believed to be Jewish owned property, and the streets and pavements of German cities were littered with the glass from previously earmarked Jewish shops, that the authorities realized what they had done. Because the great majority of the destroyed properties were in fact not owned by Jews at all, but rented by Jewish proprietors from 'German' owners, these would now be entitled to claim compensation from their insurance companies for the damage caused by this one night's rampage. The resultant compensation bill was likely to run into Millions of Marks -in fact the estimated damage bill eventually exceeded the total asset value of all the insurance companies in Germany at the time. Notwithstanding the wanton destruction of Jewish property that night, it was the events in Berlin and other German cities immediately following November 9th, which forced

71

the government to take immediate and drastic action. After only one night's organised carnage, most German insurance companies now faced certain ruin and bankruptcy. There was simply no way they could meet such a huge number of simultaneous financial claims by thousands of German shop owners against the Nazi authorities. This massive financial shortfall was especially serious for the economy as a whole. Not only had the German insurance industry invested heavily in foreign companies, but also foreign banks, especially those in America and Britain had big stakes in the booming German armament industry. * It is particularly sad that Jewish bankers both in the US and Germany also had major financial interests in the Nazi armament program. (See foot note Page 47). It was therefore essential for the government to prevent any overseas repercussions which might cause concern in Wall Street banks and to maintain an acceptable trading relationship with these foreign financiers. The truth about the Reichskristallnacht had to be hidden at all cost and the events of November 9th were therefore portrayed by the Nazi Propaganda Minister Dr.Josef Göbbels to the outside world as *"a spontaneous expression of outrage by the German people against the Jews, without any prior government knowledge or approval"*. Here then, was a disaster situation in the making which the government had simply not foreseen and was quite unprepared for.

Surprisingly, this propaganda ruse actually worked to some extent and except in America, the *'incidence of November 9th'*, was by and large seen as 'a strictly German internal affair' and apart from some incidental press reports, there was generally only limited response from the international press and community.

This was however only the beginning of Nazi woes! Most of the insurance claims were for new shop front windows and shop fittings and there was no factory in Europe capable of fulfilling a replacement 'rush order' for of such a vast quantity of heavy glass in less than six months. Most importantly, where was the money coming from to pay for all this damage and to compensate the German shop owners for the enormous financial loss to their businesses? Clearly, with the German insurance industry at the point of collapse, the replacement costs for 7500 destroyed shops would have to be addressed as soon as

---

Note: * For a detailed analysis of this collusion and a complete transcript on the internet *see "Wall Street And The Rise of Hitler".* by Anthony C.Sutton; *Bloomfield Books, London*; 1976 (reprt. 2000)

possible. The burning question: *"Who was going to pay the bill for this one night's rampage"*, now became number one priority for the Nazi hierarchy. In planning the destruction of Jewish properties, no one had considered the logistics of such a massive glass and property replacement operation.

Pondering over a possible solution, even the Nazi leaders could see they had created a real problem for themselves. But, with typical German foresight, the answer was soon to hand:

THE JEWS ARE GUILTY !

The first option was to sell on world markets all the gold and other valuables taken from Jews and looted by the S.A. from Jewish shops. However, it soon became clear that such a move would barely cover a fraction of the estimated DM 2,000,000 total damage bill. Also many of these looted items were now in the hands of persons unknown and it would be almost impossible for the State authorities to retrieve them. The question of: *"Who was going to pay for this vast amount of damage"?*, therefore remained. It was Dr. Göbbels, the government Propaganda Minister and Gauleiter of Berlin, who came up with what was considered to be ' *the perfect solution'.*

MAKE ALL JEWS PAY !!

But, how would the German public accept this latest situation? Above all, the Nazi authorities now needed an explanation with which to hoodwink the German public to take their mind off the 'official' line that there had been - *'No government involvement in the Kristallnacht carnage.'*

Conveniently, for the NAZI leadership at that time, the perfect pretext for 'making ALL the Jews pay' was found in an incident which had recently occurred in Paris. A young Polish Jew, Herschel Grynszpan, had shot Ernst Vom Rath, the 2nd Secretary at the German Embassy, a most unusual murder which had been provoked by the following tragic situation:

Whilst reading an article in a French newspaper, Herschel Grynszpan had first become aware of the terrible plight of Jewish refugees who had been forcibly evicted by Nazi troops from their homes in East Germany and were now living in the most appalling, freezing conditions in no man's land between the German and Polish borders. The Germans threatened to shoot them if they returned home, and the Polish guards threatened to shoot them if they approached their border. By chance, within days, a letter arrived from Herschel's sister in Germany, revealing that the boy's own parents were among those refugees. On reading this news, the young man's nerves simply snapped, and in his grief and anger, he set out on a campaign of revenge to kill the first high ranking German official he could find. At this point in time, he had no idea who his target would be, but as he looked at the German embassy across the road, a plan of action was slowly beginning to form in his mind. Hiding a recently purchased revolver under his coat, he made his way to the embassy and pretended to have come for the renewal of his passport. The guard on duty directed him to the 2nd Secretary at the German Embassy Ernst Vom Rath and Herschel Grynszpan, with finger on the trigger, then calmly opened the door leading to Vom Rath's office, pulled out the gun hidden under his coat and shot the Secretary several times at point blank range. Despite frantic efforts by embassy staff to save him, Vom Rath died within minutes. Herschel Grynszpan was immediately arrested by German Embassy staff and charged with murder.

This, and another shooting incident which had recently occurred in Switzerland, was just the excuse the Nazis needed to implement their diabolical plan to make all German Jews pay for the damage to Jewish properties they themselves had caused during the night of November 9th The penalty was to be DM 1Billion. (Milliarde) * *"After all"*, they reasoned, *"had not all Jews been indirectly involved in this dastardly crime against the German people, as well as in another recent shooting incident of a German official in Switzerland ?"* In the eyes of the Propaganda Minister, Dr.Josef Göbbels, ALL Jews were implicated in these crimes -and therefore ALL JEWS MUST PAY!!!

This draconian plan was to be implemented immediately in a number of carefully orchestrated stages. First, all those Jewish businesses which had not already been forced into bankruptcy, would be forced to sell their assets and business holdings to the government at rock bottom prices, then they would be robbed of any other money and invest-

---

Note: * *In today's American based fiscal terminology this would equal 1Trillion i.e.1000 Billion.*

ment holdings they still have. The government would then sell these back to the German shop owners at a huge profit, the proceeds to be returned for 'expenses' incurred by the government during the pogrom night of November 9th. Furthermore, any insurance claims for restoration and stock replacement payouts would not be paid to contracting firms, but would go directly into the coffers of the Berlin City Gauleiter, Dr.Josef Göbbels, for immediate transfer to local Nazi funds. And, best of all, this 'brilliant' plan would divert the public's attention from the official party lie of non-government involvement, and the new anti-Jewish decrees could now be presented to the German people as 'just punishment' for the complicity of the whole German-Jewish community in the 'outrageous 'murder of Secretary Vom Rath in Paris.

Immediately, this monstrous plan was put into action and before long the Nazis confiscated vast amounts of Jewish assets, imposed merciless taxes on all Jewish bank accounts and threatened the death penalty for anyone trying to transfer money or valuables to foreign banks. This gives some idea of the ruthlessness with which Jews were progressively dispossessed of any wealth and assets they still had following the implementation of earlier decrees. Minor infringements were punishable with prison, concentration camp and hard labour, and any attempt to transfer money to overseas accounts, carried the death penalty. When eventually they were forced to leave, many Jewish families, having forfeited virtually all their assets and bank accounts to the German government, finally left the country with little more than their fare and a few personal possessions.

Shocking as these details are, they represent but a fraction of the daily perils Jews had to endure under the National Socialist regime. Even all the Jewish suffering of the 1930s was merely a prelude for what all European Jews under German occupation later had to endure during the years of the Holocaust. The information is given here solely to make it easier for the reader to place him or herself mentally into the minds of these aged Jewish ex-German residents who, in their 70s and 80s had the courage to return to their homeland from every corner of the world under the banner of the German/Jewish Reconciliation Program, there to relive their unhappy childhood. As we rejoin them on the bus tour, first through the Western and then the Eastern sectors of the City, it will now be easier to comprehend their innermost thoughts and perhaps even share with them in spirit the memories of their traumatic past.

DECREES IMPOSED ON ALL JEWS BY THE NAZI GOVERNMENT DESIGNED TO DISPOSSESS THEM OF THEIR VALUABLES, ASSETS AND BANK ACCOUNTS BEFORE THEIR EXPULSION FROM GERMANY.

The Jewish Estate and Personal Possession Levy (Judenvermögensabgabegesetz)

As of November 1938, a 20% levy is to be imposed on all Jewish estates and bank accounts in lieu of their 'personal complicity' in the murder of German diplomats in Switzerland and of 2nd Secretary Vom Rath at the Paris Embassy.

The Jewish Welfare Levy (Judenwohlfahrtsteuer)

All emigrating Jews are to pay into a Jewish Pauper Fund, a 3% levy of all their estate and bank account before leaving Germany.

The State Emigration Tax (Reichsfluchtsteuer)

In addition to the Estate and Personal Levy Tax, all emigrants including non-Jews must pay to the State 25% of the value of all their estate assets and personal possessions as shown on their taxation record on January 1st 1935.

The Gold Property Tax (Goldvermögenssteuer)

All Jews must pay to the State **100%** of the value of all gold items purchased in the period 1.1.1939 –1.12.1939 and **75%** of the value of all gold items purchased _since 1933_ to the date of their departure from the Reich.

Journey To The East

T he bus now continued its tour through the suburbs of the Western sector of the City and the former Soviet DDR. Some of the highlights of this tour can be seen in photos taken from the 365 Mtr. high **Television Tower**. There was no disguising the fact that even 10 years after reunification, Berlin was in many ways still a *'divided'* city. The disparity between living standards in the affluent, US supported West and the much poorer former Soviet parts of Berlin, was most apparent. Driving through the Eastern suburbs gave an indication of what life in the former DDR under Soviet jurisdiction must have been like. Badly rendered outside walls on drab looking Soviet style apartment blocks and shabbily painted or damaged facades are reminders of long-term Communist occupation and neglect. Even eleven years after the collapse of the DDR, the remains of the infamous Berlin Wall are still evident in many places* and large areas of wasteland left by bulldozers after the demolition of the Wall stretch like unsightly scars across whole residential districts. Although, since 1989, substantial public and private investments and high priority rebuilding programs have made considerable improvements, there is still a long way to go before housing in the East will meet the stringent quality standards of those in the West. This poor building quality of workers' apartments was evident in all Eastern suburbs, an indication that just as in Russia itself, the rulers of this Communist 'utopian' workers paradise were more concerned with 'national prestige' and acquisition of personal wealth, than with providing decent housing for their people.

We also noticed some other interesting differences between East and West, such as the absence of city trams in the Western sector. The reason, we were told, is that during the reconstruction period after WW II, all trams in the Western part of Berlin were taken out of service and the areas formerly occupied by the tram lines, are now part of the green belt running down the centre of the Kurfürstendamm and other

---

Note: * Parts of the Berlin Wall have been retained to preserve some of the beautiful art work and as a reminder to future generations of the forty four years when East Germany was under Communist occupation.

City avenues.   In contrast, the trams in the former DDR have been retained and the beginnings of the tram lines now mark the entry into what was once the Soviet controlled DDR Zone. There is also an interesting difference in the pedestrian symbols on traffic lights. Whereas, in the East, the little green men actually 'walk', in the West they do not - a feature which assists strangers to the City to determine their location.

Keeping in mind that even 55 years after the collapse of Hitler's Third Reich, Berlin is still struggling to come to terms with the physical and emotional scars left by 12 years of Nazi dictatorship, it is inevitable that the legacy of 44 years of Communist rule will still be felt in Berlin for many years to come.

THE BERLIN TELEVISION TOWER

Built in the 1960's, the 365 Mtr. high Berlin Television Tower is the highest building in the capital and gives an uninterrupted 360? panoramic view of the City from a rotating platform and restaurant at 203 Mtr. above ground.

VIEWS OF WEST BERLIN

L - The <u>Berliner Dom</u> (Cathedral) as seen from the restaurant in the tower. the Cathedral is the last resting place of the Hohenzollern Dynasty and is now also used for public concerts.

R- The new Government office rise from a barren square near the Reichstag Building

VIEWS OF THE FORMER EASTERN SECTOR

L - <u>East Berlin Workers Flats.</u> Building quality in the DDR was generally of a much lower standard than in the West and the typical stereo- type Soviet style high-rise workers flats in East Berlin contrast sharply with the more traditional Western style architecture.

R - The '<u>Red Town Hall</u>' formerly in the Soviet occupied zone, derives its nickname from the locally made red bricks. It is now the Berlin Senate's Council Offices where the Jewish guests were officially welcomed by the Governing Mayor, Herr Eberhard Diepgen.

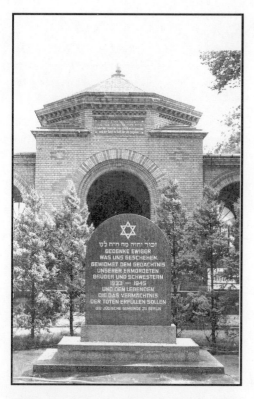

Memorial at the Weissensee Cemetery to the German Jews murdered by the Nazi government

The Plötzensee Memorial Centre

The bus made only one stop – at the **Plötzensee Memorial Centre,** a former SS prison and place of execution, which represents Nazi brutality at its worst. It was here, where General von Stauffenberg, the ring leader in the failed July 1944 assassination attempt on Adolf Hitler was executed, together with many other army officers allegedly involved in the plot. Plötzensee prison has been a place of torture and executions since well before WW II, and until its 'liberation' by Russian forces in 1945, it is estimated at least 2500 opponents of the Nazi regime were put to death here. These included Jews and members of Communist organisations, as well as many other opponents of the Third Reich. The Nazi definition of *'undesirable'*, did not only target Jews, but many non-political and religious groups including the Sinti and Roma Gypsies, Roman Catholic and Protestant priests, people who refused to cooperate on conscientious grounds such as Jehovah Witnesses, Christadelphians etc., homosexuals, lesbians and the physically and mentally handicapped. Many of those executed at Plötzensee, were also just ordinary German citizens who had been denounced by their 'neighbours' for some trivial comment regarded by the authorities as 'detrimental to Nazi Ideology'. In their fight for political freedom and human rights, some opponents of the regime had been 'activists' in the Baum anti-Nazi underground movement. (*See Page 83*). They are the heroes who chose death rather than bow to a political system whose clear intent was the destruction of the Jewish people, and everything that stands for human justice and dignity.

To orthodox Jewish visitors, who lost members of their family in the Holocaust, the experience of Plötzensee must be traumatic indeed. Here, where neither the executioner's axe nor the hangman's noose made a distinction between Jew and Gentile, the visitor to this place of death is brought face to face with the stark reality of what Nazi brutality meant to those who suffered under that system's political injustice and racial intolerance. The warning which comes out of this place of horror is not only directed to the casual visitor. Plötzensee passes moral judgment on the whole German nation and in a wider sense also on the world

81

community. As long as governments continue to treat their political and racial opponents with the same contempt as the Nazis did with the Jews and other minorities, they too stand condemned before the shrines of remembrance at the Plötzensee Memorial Centre. From here, the voices of all murdered victims cry out, irrespective of their race, religion or belief, to warn the living that all the evils which divide mankind in life are but transitory - the inescapable fate where both Jew and Gentile are joined together in eternity, whether victor or vanquished, friend or foe, - is ultimately *The Finality Of Death.*

A booklet, published by the German Resistance Centre, rightfully makes no distinction between the death of Jews who died in the Holocaust and Gentiles who suffered under the Nazi tyranny, when it states:

> *With this Memorial Centre, Berlin honours the millions of victims of the Third Reich who were defamed, maltreated, deprived of their freedom or murdered because of their political convictions, religious beliefs or racial ancestry ."*

With its powerful message about the futility of religious, racial, and ethnic strife, the Plötzensee Memorial Centre reaches out not only to the German conscience but also to all governments of the world. For it is here, at the place which commemorates the ultimate depth of human depravity, that the suffering of Gentiles and the death of millions of Jews are no longer seen as independent tragedies, but as the consequence of the same worldwide human evils – hate political greed and war. Plötzensee is the ultimate judge of humanity – for it condemns all men who, for the sake of political power and their own pride, plunge the nations into war and ignore the eternal Truth that all peoples of the world belong to the same human family and are created equal in the sight of God. .

THE PLÖTZENSEE MEMORIAL CENTRE

A Nation Remembers The Victims Of The Nazi Holocaust

P lötzensee was the SS prison and place of execution for hundreds of resistance fighters, Jews, members of various religious organisations and anyone accused of opposing the Nazi regime. It was also the end for almost 200 officers and other military personnel accused of being involved in the July 1944 plot to assassinate Adolf Hitler. This former place of death is now a memorial shrine to all the victims of Nazi brutality irrespective of race or religion.

Prison Entrance   The Execution Block

The Execution Chamber Before And After Restoration
Note: Victims' Uniform Jackets and Hanging Hooks

THE PLÖTZENSEE MEMORIAL CENTRE

A Nation Remembers The Victims Of The Nazi Holocaust

Memorial to all victims of the Hitler Dictatorship 1933-1945

Memorial to the Jewish victims of the Nazi Holocaust. The inscriptions indicate concentration camps where Jews were murdered.

(Auschwitz is 'Ringed').
Execution sites other than Concentration Camps are not specified.

Memorial to the murdered Baum Resistance fighters. Herbert Baum died in Plötzensee.

Meeting The Mayor Of Berlin

F or many guests, the Berlin Bus tour, especially the visit to the Plötzensee Memorial Centre, was undoubtedly an emotionally exhausting experience. The more relaxing reception at the City Council offices, the so-called '***Red Town Hall***', was therefore a welcome finale to the City tour. This famous building derives its name from the bright locally produced red bricks used in its construction. Before the official reception ceremony was opened by the Governing Mayor, Herr Eberhard Diepgen, the Jewish guests were welcomed in the large entrance hall by a children's' choir singing a medley of well known traditional Jewish and German folk songs. After their earlier emotional experience at Plötzensee, these aged Jewish ex-Berliners now listened intently, some tearfully, to this nostalgic reminder of their own childhood, bringing back some of the happier memories of the past.

Children's' Welcoming Choir at the ' Red Town Hall '

Following the recital, the Mayor officially welcomed the guests. He spoke first in English and then changed to German, using a most efficient young interpreter lady for the remainder of his address. Having been involved in similar work as interpreter in German Prisoner Of War camps in England during WW II, I was intrigued to learn that she was using a special shorthand translation 'code' from her four years university training. In my time, we had no training and no code. I could not help but be reminded of times when such specialised knowledge would have been of great benefit in my own work, especially when

85

acting as the official interpreter during court proceedings, where simultaneous translation involving German prisoners of war was sometimes required.

For me, this reception with the Governing Mayor was to be one of the highlights of the whole trip because, like all readers of *Aktuell,* I was already aware of Herr Diepgen's strong positive views on the question of Jewish reconciliation. It was therefore a great disappointment that the very poor acoustics in the hall, made it most difficult to hear him, the interpreter, or the questions posed by guests at the end. Even taking notes became somewhat of a futile exercise. Nevertheless, despite these inadequacies, the Mayor's well prepared address revealed an astute politician who knew what he wanted to say and who understood what his audience wanted to hear. After welcoming the Jewish guests and outlining the purpose of the already 35 year old German/Jewish Reconciliation Program, Herr Diepgen spoke of the important cultural and commercial influence Berlin's Jewish communities were having on the re-building of the capital and stressed the close ties which had been established over the years between these communities and the Berlin City administration. However, probably because of some questioners' inadequate knowledge of English, the Mayor's answers during question time seemed to lack the spontaneity and fervour expressed in his earlier address.

The official welcome was followed by a buffet style reception with wine and a variety of savoury and sweet delicacies, and this gave guests an opportunity to talk about matters of concern with Herr Diepgen and representatives of the press. My own conversation with the Mayor was regrettably short but, as mentioned earlier, its impact on my understanding of the *'Jewish Question'* in today's Germany was nevertheless profound.

Although, the whole bus tour had lasted barely three hours, the sad look on the faces of many Holocaust survivors clearly showed that for them, the first day and the realisation of being once again in the City of Berlin where they were born and where they had spent their childhood, had undoubtedly been an overwhelming emotional experience.

(b) -Visit to the Jewish Sites
The Weissensee Jewish Cemetery

N othing during the Berlin tour, except the experience at the Plötzensee Memorial Centre, had such a strong emotional effect on the Jewish guests as the visits to Jewish cemeteries, Holocaust memorials and synagogues – places often intimately associated with their own personal suffering. Included in the program, were Berlin's largest Jewish cemeteries at **Weissensee**, (where my own father and both my maternal grandparents are buried) and **Addas Jisroel**, the cemetery of the Israelite Synagogue Community. Both sites have memorials to the many unknown victims from Auschwitz and other camps whose remains have found their last resting place here. The huge Weissensee cemetery, formerly in the DDR covers many hectares, and like other similar Jewish sites under former Soviet jurisdiction, had been badly neglected for years. Especially noticeable were the endless avenues of grave sites still submerged in an entanglement of overgrown weeds and ivy creepers. This huge burial site is subdivided into a 'matrix' layout of mostly inadequately maintained gravel paths running in all directions with many of the path indicators at intersections rusted away, unreadable, or simply missing. Even with the map supplied to all visitors, accurate location of one's position within the cemetery, therefore becomes more a matter of guesswork than planning.

There is an interesting sequence to our previous visit to Weissensee Cemetery. After our brief stay there in 1993, I was so concerned about what appeared to me the neglected condition of the grave sites that I wrote to the directors expressing my concerns about what appeared to me a case of serious neglect on the part of the cemetery authorities. I informed them that I felt the survivors of Hitler's death camps deserved a more cared for final resting place. In due course, I received a letter back saying that they were fully aware of the situation, but were severely limited by funding and shortage of staff. If I thought Weissensee was ' *bad* ', they suggested, I should visit some other Jewish Cemeteries in the former Soviet occupied zone to see what long-term neglect can really do. I felt greatly humbled, when sometime later I read that certain areas at the Weissensee Cemetery were being *deliberately* kept in this apparently dilapidated state in memory of the many Jews and other refugees who during WW II, and again during the Soviet occupation, were able to save their lives by hiding from the authorities in this Weissensee 'jungle' of weeds and ivy entanglements.

The primary purpose of our visit to Weissensee was to locate the graves of my maternal grandparents, Dr.Wilhelm Sachs, former Professor of Dentistry at Berlin and Breslau Universities, his wife, Fredericka, and the grave of my father who died in 1938, shortly before our departure from Germany. Unfortunately, I have no personal recollections, except some photos of any of my grandparents, who all died before I was born. To assist in this quest, we had previously given details of the grave locations to the program organisers to be passed on to the cemetery authorities. However, because the data there was at that time only recorded on microfiche and not on computer, retrieval of this information turned out to be a painfully slow process. Seven years earlier in 1993, our first effort to locate these graves had ended in a two hour fruitless search in torrential rain among the ivy and weeds. So, this time, my sister's husband and self, having complied with the cemetery rules to don the traditional Jewish 'Yarmulke' head covering, and equipped with a small reference map, set out in drizzling rain to find my father's and maternal grandparents' graves. Although, we did eventually find the latter, unfortunately after 1 ½ hours, even with the assistance of a cemetery worker, the search for my father's grave in the jungle of Weissensee, again proved fruitless. In the seven years since our last visit, little seemed to have changed in this vast burial ground, except perhaps my deeper appreciation for the conditions of this, the largest Jewish cemetery in Berlin.

As I clambered through the weeds and ivy in search of my father's grave, I remembered the Jews and others who had found shelter here and I somehow even felt 'guilty' for treading on what had now become almost "Holy Ground". Still pondering over this lesson in humility, I left Weissensee, thankful that at least we had been able to take a photo of my grandparents' gravesite and that my wife, my only sister and her husband had been able to share this unique experience together.(See Page 89).

On the way out, we met two other couples from our group who had also been unable to find the grave of their loved ones. Because the Weissensee visit was only scheduled for two hours and having walked almost three kilometres in drizzling rain, we finally gave up, tired and ready for the bus trip back to the hotel. As we boarded the bus, we noticed a discreetly positioned police security vehicle at the entrance gate, a reassuring 'precaution' we witnessed not only at Weissensee, but also at all other Jewish memorial sites and synagogues we visited.

MEMORIAL PLAQUE AT THE WEISSENSEE
JEWISH CEMETERY

Memorial Plaque at the entrance
to the Weissensee Jewish Cemetery

REMEMBER ALWAYS WHAT HAPPENE4D TO US
DEDICATED TO THE MEMORY OF OUR MURDERED
BROTHERS AND SISTERS
1933 – 1945
AND THE LIVING
WHO MUST NOW CARRY OUT
THE WILL OF THOSE WHO DIED

The Jewish Communities in Berlin

THE WEISSENSEE JEWISH CEMETERY

Police Security Car-
at the cemetery gates

Was this the creeping weeds and ivy
jungle where Jews and gentiles hid
from persecution?

The author and his sister at their grandparents' grave

Visit To Other Jewish Memorial Sites

Sites Visited - ●   Sites Not Visited - ☆

N owhere, is there greater evidence of Germany's resolve to *'hold out the olive branch'* to returning Jews, than the official policy not to 'whitewash' the terrible events of the Nazi era. This policy has taken on a number of directions:

❖ Ongoing 'official' reminders regarding Germany's responsibility for atrocities and persecution of the Jews under the Nazi dictatorship.

❖ Continuing official support for returning Jews and the Jewish communities.

❖ Erection of memorials to remind the public of Nazi atrocities committed against Jews and other minorities during the Holocaust era.

❖ Ongoing support by the Federal government for financial compensation to all ex-German Jews who suffered under the Nazi regime.

❖ Provision for Jewish ex-concentration camp inmates to establish dialogue with German schools and families.

❖ Encouragement by German educational authorities for high school students to be aware of the true facts regarding the Nazi persecution of the Jews and other minorities.

Wherever one looks in *'The New Berlin'*, there is a reminder that more than fifty five years after the liberation of the death camps, the subject of Hitler's attempt to destroy the Jewish presence in Europe, is still one of the most discussed topics in Germany today - in newspapers, on Television and even in current (year 2000) theatre productions like *"Ich bin's nicht – Adolf Hitler ist es gewesen"* (*"It's not me – it was Adolf Hitler"*), which at the time of our visit had already recorded over 3000 performances. It is impossible to escape from this reality, for the reminders of this monstrous crime described by former Bundespresident Roman Herzog at the 1999 Day Of Commemoration For The Victims Of The Nazi Holocaust as *"Our Common And Most Terrible Inheritance"*

(*Aktuell 65/1999, p31*), are present throughout the Federal Republic, especially the capital Berlin. As the Bundespresident says, "*The legacy left by 12 years of Nazi dictatorship is not only indelibly engraved in stone and iron memorials in Berlin and other cities throughout the Federal Republic - it is also etched deeply into the consciousness of the German people themselves as a permanent reminder and warning to every new generation of the moral dangers inherent in political non-vigilance.*"

But above all, that '*Common And Most Terrible Inheritance*' will be permanently enshrined in the massive national memorial to the 6,000,000 Jewish victims who perished in the Holocaust, to be erected right in the centre of the capital Berlin, that City where in 1942 the Nazi Party planned the extermination of the entire Jewish population of Europe. To locate this stain of national dishonour in the very centre of the national capital, the place where the brutal, uncompromising Nazi racial ideology was first formulated, must surely rank among the politically most courageous decisions of all time. In order to really appreciate the importance of that decision, one has to see the very existence of this memorial not only as a witness to the 6,000,000 Jewish victims of Nazi brutality, but also as a manifestation of the German peoples' moral courage and spiritual greatness. Let the reader reflect here for a moment, and ask him or herself: "*Where else, but in Germany, are there shrines of remembrance which so uncompromisingly condemn atrocities organized and executed by a former State government? Where else in the world has a national government had the political will to construct such a prominent edifice of national shame in their own capital?* But most importantly, this memorial has to be seen as a permanent warning to future German generations, and indeed the world, what can happen when ordinary citizens become _willing_ participants in cohort with a government driven by lust for power and economic greed. Here is a forceful reminder how easily ordinary law abiding citizens can be manipulated by an evil minded regime to condone and participate in the most terrible crimes against the innocent.

The Berlin Holocaust Memorial has therefore to be seen as the ultimate act of national self-incrimination and proof of the peoples' genuine determination to learn from and atone for their violent past. By its very existence, this shrine of remembrance witnesses to the world that the murder of the 6,000,000 Jews here remembered, *will never be erased from the national conscience or ever be accepted as having been politically justified.* It is to the credit of German governments that they recognize and accept - it is their moral responsibility to prevent a reoccurrence of the Nazi Holocaust by permanently keeping that memory alive and remembering Germany's shameful past. In dealing with that past and especially 'The Jewish Question', there are no excuses for 'whitewashing' –! Here, at the foot of this national shrine, and indeed in the presence of all Holocaust memorials, the visitor is brought face to face with the full horror of Nazi brutality - the fear and humiliation of the victims, the families ripped apart, the mass arrests, the enforced marches through city streets, the horrendous transport in cattle trucks to the extermination camps in the East - and finally the systematic murder of millions of innocent people whose only crime was being born Jews.

.But besides this important message to German youth, this shrine of remembrance has also a very special meaning for all who became the victims of Nazi persecution – namely *this* - that in this unique manifestation of national atonement, 55 years after Auschwitz, there is now an opportunity for Jews and Germans to move forward in the reconciliation process. Coming to terms with this memorial, may be seen as the first step. Jewish readers might therefore reflect for a moment on the extraordinary political courage shown by the German government and the people of Berlin, in erecting this shrine in such a prominent location in the very heart of the capital as a permanent witness to the nation's ultimate debt not only to the 6,000,000 Jews who perished, but also to the survivors. I believe that to regard this memorial as anything else, fails to give credence to its importance as part of the ongoing German/Jewish healing process. This is the message of hope that must now not only be passed on to the children and grandchildren of the Jewish survivors, but also to the children and grandchildren of every new German generation. Only by ongoing dialogue at the personal level between Jewish and German Youth in an atmosphere of mutual respect, trust and understanding, can the hatred and suspicion created by long-term negative thinking be changed. The youth of tomorrow, irrespective of race or colour of skin are after all, the future of *all* mankind and the torch bearers for the survival of the human race as a whole.

Not only this memorial, but many other memorials throughout the Federal Republic proclaim anew to the world that the heart of this nation has changed. For instance, in Rüdesheim, a small town on the River Rhein, we saw a memorial plaque in memory of the Israelite Religious Community's Synagogue destroyed by the Nazis on November 11th 1938, shortly after the Reichskristallnacht.

> **Die Synagoge der Israelitischen Religions-gesellschaft Rüdesheim – Gelsenheim stand von 1843 - 1938 an der gegenüberliegenden Straßenseite. Sie wurde am 11. November 1938 nach der Pogromnacht zerstört.**

The Synagogue of the Rüdesheim/Gelsenheim Israelite Religious Community stood here on the opposite side of the street from 1843 to 1938. The building was destroyed on 11th November 1938, after the Reichskristallnacht.

THE MEMORIAL FOUNDATION
FOR THE MURDERED JEWS OF EUROPE

Following a resolution by the German Bundestag and in accordance with the design submitted by the Jewish architect Peter Eisenmannn, the Foundation will erect on this site a memorial for the 6,000,000 European Jews murdered by the Nazi government in the years 1930 - 1945.

Proposed Memorial Site for the 6,000,000
Jewish victims of the Nazi Holocaust

This project commemorating the Jewish victims of the Nazi Holocaust is a unique gesture of goodwill by the German government and the people - a permanent reminder to all future generations of the terror which was Hitler's 'Final Solution For The Jewish Problem In Europe' - The planned extermination of all Jews and their ancient culture.

As I watched the faces of the guests at the Jewish memorial sites, I felt deeply for those members of our group who had lost their loved ones in Hitler's concentration camps, in some cases even their entire families. How thankful we are that our own family had been spared that fate! But despite their grief, we could sense that 55 years after the liberation of the camps, a few guests seem to be slowly coming to terms with their traumatic past. As we watched these elderly Jews, standing at the foot of the Levetzowstrasse Memorial, *(See Front Cover)*, deep in their private world, searching for a *'spiritual bridge'* between themselves and the family members they had lost, I could not help wondering how many could see in this memorial also a symbol of the longing for forgiveness by the German people reaching out to those whom their forefathers had so dreadfully wronged. Such an 'extended' view of the new German/Jewish relationship requires the acceptance of these sites *for what they really represent* - not only a permanent reminders of Germany's violent past, but also a symbolic manifestation of the German peoples' change of heart towards returned Jews and Jews still in the Diaspora.

Overall view of the Berlin Holocaust Memorial to the 6,000,000 Jews murdered in the Nazi Holocaust , inaugurated in May 2005

The Levetzowstrasse Memorial And Beyond

No site we visited, except the Plötzensee Memorial Centre, had such a traumatic effect on the Jewish guest as that at the former **Levetzowstrasse Synagogue,** shown on the cover of this book. Like many similar places of worship, during WW II, this House of God was used by the SS as an assembly hall for thousands of Jews destined for extermination in the East. The **Levetzowstrasse Memorial** commemorates the 40 out of 63 cattle wagon transports which between October 1941 and April 1945 took 55,696 Berlin Jewish men, women and children for what under the Nazi racial cleansing program was termed *'Resettlement in the East',* a euphemism for deportation either to one of the city ghettos in Poland or directly to Hitler's extermination camps. After their arrest, and having been forced out of their homes at gunpoint in the middle of the night, countless Jewish families were either force marched or transported in trucks to the Levetzowstrasse synagogue site and other assembly points. After a brutal body search and 'registration' by the SS, families were taken to the nearest railway goods yards at the Pulitzer or the Anhalter railway station, where they were herded into cattle trucks and transferred to the rail siding # 17 at the Grunewald rail depot for the journey to their 'final destination'. *(See Page 106).*

It was in fact the meticulous transportation records kept by the SS **(using the American IBM punch card documentation system)** which in post-war investigations, not only facilitated the search for missing persons, but, in some cases, also with the help of the Simon Wiesenthal records, brought at least some former members of the SS to justice. Diligent SS record keeping (except for those Jews destined for the gas chambers who were considered merely as 'expendable vermin' by the Nazis), has also made it possible for many of the deported Berlin Jews to be identified by name. Every year on January 27th, the anniversary of the liberation of Auschwitz, their names are read out at the Grunewald rail depot siding # 17 and other sites in the City of Berlin. And so, the list of Jewish deportees the Nazis had classified as 'undesirable' and ' of no value to the State ',grew from day to day - men, women and children, including the old, the infirm and babes in arms, destined to become mere statistics in the Nazi drive to destroy the Jewish presence in Europe.

For the majority, life eventually ended in the gas chambers of Auschwitz-Birkenau or at the Treblinka, Sobibor or Chelmo extermination camps. Transports came from Germany and from every country in Nazi occupied Europe. Most trains heading East first stopped at *Theresienstadt* (Terezin), a concentration camp in Czechoslovakia which the Nazis had turned into a Jewish 'Ghetto City'. From here, tens of thousands of Jews were then transported to Auschwitz, and other destinations.

But the planned destruction of Europe's Jews was not confined to Hitler's death camps – many of his victims already succumbed to starvation, disease and cold on the journey to the camps, were shot or were simply left to die at the road side on one of the terrible death marches following the closing of Auschwitz and other camps in January 1945 in the wake of the advancing Soviet Army. It is estimated that on these marches alone, at least 100,000 Jews and other *'undesirables'* perished. Any poor soul, too exhausted to continue the cruel march in the bitter cold, was simply shot on the spot by the Nazi guards and left to die at the road side. In the early stages of the 'Final Solution Program', Jewish deportees were also sent direct to Latvia and Lithuania, there to be shot in their thousands and buried in huge mass graves. Not surprising that knowing the fate which awaited them, many deportees, no longer able to endure these inhumane conditions, sought their last rest in suicide. German, as well as Jewish records testify that between 1940 and 1945, almost 6,000,000 Jews from every country in Europe occupied by German forces perished in the Nazi drive to make the continent *'Judenrein'* – i.e. 'cleansed of all Jews'. In Poland alone, where in some communities over 90% of the pre-war Jewish population perished, the toll is estimated to have exceeded 2,000,000.

As the extermination program continued unabated, mass shootings proved *'too slow and inefficient'* for the Nazi killing machine. A *'more efficient method'* had to be found! The next step in the extermination of *'undesirables'* was *'Trial Killings'* in specially sealed vans using Carbon Monoxide gas, a gas that had already achieved what the Nazis called,' *considerable success'* before the war in special State institutions on mentally and physically handicapped inmates, including many children. These van trials ultimately led to the development of a more 'effective' form of the highly toxic agent Zyklon B, originally developed for the extermination of rodents.

It is interesting to recall here that during the pre-war period, it was a deliberate Nazi policy to depict all Jews as '**Vermin**' – no more worthy to exist than rats. A well known propaganda film showed a rat infested wheat barn and left no doubt in the viewer's mind that Jews were no better than pest carrying rodents. The message was clear:

> # "JEWS ARE LIKE RATS – DESTROY THEM WHEREVER YOU FIND THEM!"

With typical German efficiency, the further development of this poison gas proved no problem for the Nazi hierarchy. Improvements in quality and better sealing of the gas chambers were soon hailed as the *'perfect method'* for mass extermination at Auschwitz –Birkenau and other death camps. It was Hitler's ultimate weapon in his *"Final Solution for the Jewish Problem in Europe"*. In August 1943 these mass killings reached their climax when, according to SS records, in one single day over 10,000 Jews and other *'undesirables'* were murdered in the *'now perfected'* gas chambers of Auschwitz-Birkenau and other camps, the whole operation as usual being 'watched with gleeful satisfaction by the SS guards through gas sealed windows. On hearing of this improved development, Heinrich Himmler, Head of the SS and Adolf Eichman, the Chief Executive of the 'Final Solution Program', were almost beside themselves for joy. At last, they had the means to carry out the Führer's ultimate plan to save the German people from the scourge of the Zionist threat and make the whole of Europe *'Judenrein'*.

And the greatest irony is that the last thing the Jewish men, women and children saw as they were being herded into the gas chambers was the motto embossed on the belt buckles of the SS guards. It said:

"GOTT MIT UNS " – God With Us.

Mountains of shoes and clothing taken from over 10,000 Jews destined for the gas chambers. At the height of the 'Final Solution Program' , this represented ONE DAY"s mass killings of what the Nazis considered no more than " vermin "

THE PRE-WAR LEVETZOWSTRASSE SYNAGOGUE

The former Levetzowstrasse Jewish Synagogue. Like many other places of worship, this House Of God was used by the Nazis as a pre-deportation assembly area for Jewish families destined for the extermination camps in the East.

The magnificent pre-war interior of Berlin's largest Jewish synagogue in the Rykestrasse, typical of many places of worship in the capital and other German cities destroyed in the pogrom night of November 9th 1938 and allied bombing.

But let us now return to the site of the former Levetzowstrasse Synagogue, where so many Berlin Jews started their 'Journey to Auschwitz' and other camps, and consider the circumstances which led to the erection of this unusual memorial. The situation is especially interesting, because it is again indicative of the deep sense of shame still felt by many Germans today regarding the events relating to the Nazi persecution of the Jewish people. For many years after the war, only a simple bronze wall plaque marked the location where once stood one of Berlin's most famous Jewish synagogues. But, in the 1980's, the decision was made that such an unobtrusive plaque was inadequate and that a new, much more meaningful edifice should be erected on the former Synagogue site in recognition of the magnitude of the crime perpetrated here. The result was a 'three phase' memorial, made up of (1) - a massive *six Mtr. long steel plate,* recording the date, number and destinations of the thousands of transported Jews, *(See Front Cover)*; (2) - *A replica of a cattle wagon,* rammed into a huge granite stone block as a reminder of the terrible train journey to the death camps which started from this site, and (3)- *36 bronze plaques* cemented into the ground, each with a description of the history and destruction of a Berlin Jewish Synagogue destroyed by the Nazis or by allied bombing during WW II.

● STAGE 1 OF THE LEVETZOWSTRASSE SYNAGOGUE MEMORIAL

The Steel plate with the laser cut names, dates and destinations of the thousands of Jews who were deported from this former House of Worship and murdered in Auschwitz and other camps in the East.

● STAGE 2 OF THE LEVETZOWSTRASSE SYNAGOGUE MEMORIAL

Replica of a cattle wagon similar to the ones used by the Nazis to transport thousands of Jews to the death camps from German occupied countries in Europe. The Granite block is a reminder of the terribly cramped conditions endured by the Jews during their final journey

● STAGE 3 OF THE LEVETZOWSTRASSE SYNAGOGUE MEMORIAL

Section of the floor plate memorial commemorating the destruction of 36 Berlin synagogues and prayer houses by the Nazis or by allied bombing in WW II.

- ## THE LEVETZOWSTRASSE SYNAGOGUE
  ## MEMORIAL PLAQUE

TRANSLATION OF PLAQUE INSCRIPTION

On this site once stood one of Berlin's largest Synagogues.   In 1941, the Berlin Jewish community was forced by the SS to convert the building into a pre-deportation assembly area.   From here, more than 37,500 Berlin Jews were transported to the extermination camps via the Grunewald and Pulitzerstrasse goods depots.   In addition, between 6.6.1942 and 27.3.1945, a further 14,797 Jews in 117 transports were deported to the Theresienstadt concentration camp via the Anhalter Bahnhof railway station from the second largest assembly area in Berlin, the former Jewish retirement home in the Grosse Hamburgerstrasse. During the pogrom night of November 9th 1938, the so-called Reichskristallnacht, all Jewish places of worship were damaged, burnt or totally destroyed by the National Socialists. Symbolic of the long established Jewish culture, synagogues became the direct target for the State organised terror. Besides the names of the synagogues here remembered, there were over 80 Jewish prayer houses and other places of worship, all of which became either targets for destruction during the Reichskristallnacht of November 9th 1938, or were later sold, closed or taken over by the State.

The full horror of this place and what happened here, does however not really strike home until one appreciates what was involved in the actual creation of such a plate memorial. The choice of the material used in its construction is especially significant because the deliberate use of raw steel which naturally deteriorates with exposure to the elements, forcefully conveys the idea of *'physical destruction'*. Furthermore, unlike bronze and copper, raw steel is by its very nature unsuitable for engraving. Looking from the front, as seen on page 99 and the front cover of this book, the details of each transport i.e. dates, deportation 'quantity' and destination, can be clearly seen through the massive thick plate, indicating that the volume of metal for each letter and number must have been literally *'burnt out'* with a laser cutter - a powerful symbolic reminder of the brutality unleashed by the SS against the thousands of innocent Jewish men, women and children who were sent to the death camps from this former House of God. Let the reader pause here for a moment and consider the thoughts and feelings which must have gone through the mind of the steel worker who created this memorial as he slowly burnt each letter and number into that steel plate whilst reflecting on the nature and purpose of his task.

Railroad to Hell ! The Auschwitz disembarkation platform (known as 'Die Judenrampe'), is on the right with the entrance to the concentration camp in the far distance. Trains often arrived in the early hours of the morning, a time when the deportees were emotionally and physically at their lowest ebb.

"Selection" on the *Judenrampe*, May/June 1944. To be sent to the right meant assignment to a work detail; to the left, the gas chambers. This image shows the arrival of Hungarian Jews from Carpatho-Ruthenia, many of them from the Berehov ghetto

☆ NO. 17 RAIL SIDING AT THE GRUNEWALD RAILWAY STATION

N o. 17 Siding at the Grunewald Railway Station, West Berlin, was the embarkation point used by the SS to load more than 55,600 Jewish men ,women and children from Berlin and the surrounding districts into cattle transport wagons – destined for the extermination camps at Auschwitz, Theresienstadt, Treblinka, Sobibor, Riga and other destinations in the East. In the Nazi racial ideology, there was no distinction made between children of all ages and even tiny babies were classed as 'being of no value to the State' and therefore destined for destruction in the gas chambers. As far as is known, only a small number of Berlin Jews who were sent to the camps, survived. A memorial now reminds weekend picnickers to this beautiful area of Grunewald lakes and pines of the terrible events which took place here between October 1941 and April 1945.

The infamous rail siding # 17 at the Grunewald Rail Depot where "The Journey To Hell" began for more than 55,600 Berlin Jews.

The terrible journey to Auschwitz and other camps in the East begins for the deported Jews of Europe.

☆ THE GRUNEWALD RAIL SIDING # 17 MEMORIAL SITE

B ased on meticulously detailed SS records of every person transported, every year at this location, on the anniversary of the Holocaust Memorial Day, the names are read out in public of all Jews who started their final journey to the East from the Grunewald rail siding # 17,

BERLIN TO AUSCHWITZ

Here, the terrible journey to Auschwitz and other camps
in the East began for the deported Berlin Jews

Jewish officials at the 1998 Inauguration Ceremony at the Grunewald Railyard
Memorial Siding # 17

Two other Jewish synagogues included in the program were the **Rykestrasse Synagogue**, once Germany's largest, now mostly restored after being almost totally destroyed during the war, the Synagogue in the **Grosse Hamburgerstrasse** and the **Neue Synagogue** with its associated **Centrum Judaicum Exhibition: "Jews in Berlin 1938 – 1945"**. The display includes a wide range of exhibits, documents, newspaper cuttings and artefacts relating to the Jewish persecution during the Nazi period 1933 -1945. Of particular interest was the inscription below on a marble plaque at the exhibition entrance, which expresses and reflects today's positive attitude of the Berlin Jewish community.

● MARBLE PLAQUE AT THE ENTRANCE
TO THE NEUE SYNAGOGUE

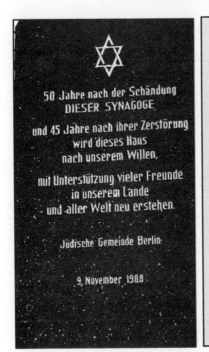

50 Jahre nach der Schändung
DIESER SYNAGOGE

und 45 Jahre nach ihrer Zerstörung
wird dieses Haus
nach unserem Willen,

mit Unterstützung vieler Freunde
in unserem Lande
und aller Welt neu erstehen.

Jüdische Gemeinde Berlin

9. November 1988

TRANSLATION

50 years after the desecration of this Synagogue and 45 years after its destruction, it is our determination that with the help of many friends in our country and the world

THIS HOUSE

WILL RISE AGAIN

The Jewish Community
Of Berlin
9th November 1988

The notorious entrance gate to Auschwitz Concentration Camp bears the inscription "WORK MAKES YOU FREE. Within three hours of passing through this gate, most internees had been either allocated to work as slave laborers, or murdered in the gas chambers

The Terrible Inheritance That Cannot Be Erased"

I t is most significant that throughout Germany, memorials erected at sites where Nazi atrocities were committed, are classified not merely as '***Denkmahle'*** i.e. '**Commemorative Sites**' but as '***Mahnmale'*** that is -'**Warning Sites**' – forceful reminders, especially to German youth, that as the future decision makers, they carry not only the moral responsibility to remember and learn from that shameful Nazi era in German history, but also to prevent its reoccurrence. Because, there are so many memorials in Berlin recalling the Nazi period, it is impossible to go far in this city without being confronted with this nation's past atrocities against the Jewish people. Unfortunately, because of the limited time available, some of the sites listed below (marked ★) could not be visited in the short seven days we were in the capital. I believe however, that because of their special significance, these memorial sites also deserve mention and they have therefore been included here. Visited sites are marked ●

- ● Berlin's Oldest Jewish Cemetery
- ● The Former Jewish Retirement Home
- ● The Rosenstrasse Memorial
- ★ The Koppenplatz Memorial
- ★ The Wittenberg Underground Station Memorial
- ★ The Steglitz Memorial
- ★ The Book Burning Memorial
- ★ The House Of The Wannsee Conference

☆ THE MEMORIAL AT THE ENTRANCE TO THE WITTENBERG UNDERGROUND STATION

T his memorial in the City centre is in the form of a large plaque, outside the entrance to the **Wittenbergplatz Underground Station** and lists twelve concentration camps to which Berlin's Jews were deported - Auschwitz heads the list, a daily reminder to thousands of Berlin commuters on their way to the office, of the Jewish men, women and children who were deported to these camps by the Nazi government, there to be brutally murdered . *Heading the plaque is the grim warning:*

"These Are The Places Of Horror Which We Must Never Be Allowed To Forget"

Auschwitz	Stutthof	Majdanek
Treblinka	Theresienstadt	Buchenwald
Dachau	Sachsenhausen	Ravensbrück
Bergen -Belsen	Trostenez	Flossenbürg

ENTRANCE AND PLAQUE AT THE WITTENBERG UNDERGROUND STATION

 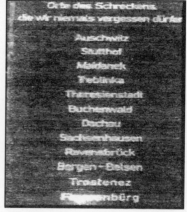

● BERLIN'S OLDEST JEWISH CEMETERY

T he visit to **Berlin's oldest Jewish cemetery,** founded in 1671, was another reminder of the authorities' resolve to keep the past alive. A large plaque reminds the visitor that in 1943 the Gestapo (Secret Police) ploughed up the area and that hundreds of civilians, who died during the final Allied assault on Berlin, are now buried here. Miraculously, almost the only original grave stone left standing is that of the famous philosopher and founder of the Jewish reform movement Moses Mendelssohn, who died in 1786.

TRANSLATION OF PLAQUE

"In memory of the oldest burial site of the Berlin Jewish Community. This cemetery was in use from 1672 – 1827 and was destroyed in 1943 on the orders of the Gestapo"

Grave Stone Of Moses Mendel-ssohn, famous 18th Century philosopher and founder of the Jewish reform movement. The inscription is in German, and in Hebrew.

● THE FORMER JEWISH RETIREMENT HOME

I n close proximity to the cemetery, stood the oldest *Jewish Retirement Home in Berlin*. Like the Levetzowstrasse Synagogue, this place was also used by the Nazis as a '*Sammellager*', an assembly area for Jews earmarked for deportation to the death camps. The building was badly damaged in WW II air raids and later demolished. Since 1996, every year on the anniversary of the Holocaust Day of Remembrance the 55,696 names of deported Berlin Jews are read out here in public. At the entrance there are two striking memorials which recall this era of Jewish suffering. The first is a plaque mounted on a granite monument with the following inscription:

TRANSLATION OF PLAQUE

This marks the site of the first Jewish Community Retirement Home in Berlin. In 1942, the Gestapo turned the house into a deportation assembly area for Jewish citizens. 55,000 Berlin Jews, including infants and the aged, were deported to the concentration camps at Auschwitz and Theresienstadt, there to be brutally murdered.

NEVER FORGET WHAT HAPPENED HERE !
FIGHT AGAINST WAR
GUARD THE PEACE

● THE FORMER JEWISH RETIREMENT HOME

Another memorial is in the form of a bronze sculpture of nine bedraggled human figures representing the deportation to the death camps of thousands of Jewish women and children from this site.

☆ THE KOPPENPLATZ MEMORIAL

Although, not actually in the program, some guests went to see another reminder of the past, not far from the former retirement home. This memorial is in the Koppenplatz Public Park with the unusual title *"Der Verlassene Raum"* (literally " The room that was [had to be] suddenly vacated "). The large floor display consists of an antique table and an overturned chair, reminders of the time when thousands of Berlin Jews, living in constant fear of arrest, often had to flee their homes at short notice. Anytime, day or night, a knock on the door could mean arrest, deportation and death and this memorial recalls the suddenness with which such events could strike. Erected in 1996, the memorial was the winning entry in a 1998 competition on the 60th anniversary of the Reichskristallnacht on November 9th 1938.

● THE ROSENSTRASSE MEMORIAL

I nteresting also is the story behind the memorial erected in 1995 in memory of the so-called *"Women Protesters in the Rosenstrasse"*. Until early 1943, there were still 27,000 Jews in Berlin, most of them employed as forced labour in war production plants. In February that year, the SS arrested 7000 for deportation to the death camps. Among these were men married to 'Arian Germans', which made them *'Category Two'* citizens in the Nazi code of racial classification. These men were not immediately deported, but interned in a former Jewish welfare building in the Rosenstrasse. Hearing about their men's arrest, several hundred wives and mothers began a 12 days peaceful demonstration in protest against the arrest of their men folk. Fearing a wider protest, Nazi authorities eventually released the men. As far as it is known, this was the only occasion when the SS actually bowed to the demands of public demonstrators. After their release, at least some of these Jews were able to escape abroad with false passports, or save themselves by hiding from the SS, (perhaps even in the "jungle" of the Weissensee Cemetery ??)

Stone sculpture of the Jewish men who were to be sent to Auschwitz for extermination by the Gestapo, but were saved by their brave women who protested against their deportation.

●THE ROSENSTRASSE MEMORIAL

Stone sculpture of the women who staged the demonstration in the Rosenstrasse on October 18th 1943 to save their men folk from arrest and deportation by the Gestapo.

INAUGURATION OF THE ROSENSTRASSE MEMORIAL
OCTOBER 18th 1995

At the Inauguration Ceremony of the memorial on October 18th 1995, a witness to the demonstrations remembers the dramatic events in the Rosenstrasse on October 18th 1943.

☆ THE STEGLITZ MEMORIAL

Further afield, in the suburb of Steglitz is an unusual **Wall Of Remembrance**. This is a 12 Mtr. long polished Chrome steel plate, engraved with the names and deportation details of 1723 Jews transported by the SS from this Berlin suburb to Auschwitz. The memorial is particularly interesting because the reflective mirror effect of the polished Chrome steel surface gives the illusion of a physical blending of the 'Real World', and the deported Jews whose names are engraved on the memorial.

This unusual memorial in the suburb of Steglitz commemorates the 1723 Jews transported by the SS to Auschwitz concentration camp from here during the years of the Holocaust

Unveiling of the Steglitz Memorial

Note: The 'blending effect' created by the polished Chrome steel surface giving the illusion of the 'Living' in the real world merging' with the inscriptions of the dead.

⭐ THE BURNING OF THE BOOKS 1933 & 1935
THE NAZI ATTEMPT TO DESTROY JEWISH CULTURE

I n 1933 and again in 1935, the Nazis unleashed their fury against Jewish writers and intellectuals when thousands of ire-placeable Jewish writings and works of art were classified as '*UnGerman Literature*', and destroyed in massive bonfires throughout the Third Reich. In this act of desecration, original manuscripts by the great composers Mendelssohn, Mahler, and others disappeared for ever in the flames. Literary works by Thomas Mann, Erich Kästner (an opponent writer of the Nazi regime) ,Voltaire, Lessing, Heine, Marx, Engels, Freud and many other Jewish and 'liberal' writers succumbed to the same fate. In the post-war period, this destruction by the Nazis of Jewish art and writings is remembered each year on May 10th, the anniversary of the burning, at all those sites where the destruction took place. It is interesting here to recall that the burning of Jewish literature by the Nazis was not the first time this had occurred in Germany. Witnessing a similar act of destruction of Jewish literature in **1817**, the well known Jewish writer Heinrich Heine, uttered. these prophetic words:

> " Where Today They Burn Books, Tomorrow They Will Burn People"

How terribly true this prediction became in the belching smoke of the Auschwitz crematoria.

Burning Of Jewish Books 1935

Memorial Service at a Berlin Book Burning Site

117

★ THE WANNSEE - LAKE OF BEAUTY AND RECREATION

Every year, thousands of Berliners flock to their favourite recreational areas West of the City, where the two rivers Spree and Havel converge to form an extensive inlet lake and water system. At the heartland of these lovely surroundings is Lake Wannsee and the enchanting Grunewald forest. The most popular recreational area is the Lake environment with its excellent swimming and boating facilities, a favourite escape from the pressures of City life for Berliners who come to this beautiful area to enjoy a walk in the nearby Grunewald forest or to take a boat trip on the lake. The pictures below give an indication of this idyllic family recreation area within easy reach of one of the largest cities in Europe.

Berliners enjoying the
beautiful Lake Wannsee

A haven for Boats and
Family Outings

Sailing On The River Havel

☆ THE WANNSEE - LAKE OF HORROR AND DEATH

But in 1942, the Nazis turned Berlin's favourite recreational area into a place of indescribable horror. Following an earlier SS census of Jews in all the occupied countries, senior Nazi officials met on January 20th 1942, near the beautiful Lake Wannsee in a large private mansion, now known as *"The House Of The Wannsee Conference "* to authorize and initiate Hitler's 'Final Solution Program' for the systematic extermination of 11,000,000 European Jews. As was shown earlier, under this viciously orchestrated genocide program, the nearby Grunewald Rail siding # 17 became the embarkation point for more than 55,600 Berlin Jews earmarked for extermination in the death camps of the East.

In 1947, the complete minutes of that meeting as recorded by Adolf Eichmann, the organizer and executioner of 'The Final Solution Program', were found in the files of the German Foreign Office. After the war, the building previously used as a recreational facility by the SS and the Gestapo, was occupied by both American and Russian forces. Since 1992 the Wannsee House has been a public shrine of remembrance with an extensive library, a permanent exhibition and study centre dealing with all aspects of racial intolerance, but especially analysing the Nazi persecution of the Jews under the National Socialists.

The Infamous House Of The Wannsee Conference

Here, in January 1942, Hitler's 'Final Solution for the Jewish Problem' was implemented – the annihilation of the entire European Jewish population of 11,000,000 men, women and children.

GERMANY'S FEDERAL LADY CHANCELLOR
AND PRESIDENT OF THE BUNDESTAG

Frau Angela Merkel (CDU) – Germany's first Lady Chancellor. Under her leadership, the German Bundestag now governs the Federal Parliament in a coalition of the' right' , the CDU and the 'left' the SPD

Dr. Wolfgang Thierse, (SPD) - Presdent of the German Parliament.   In May 2005, he officially opened the Berlin Holocaust Memorial to the public.

(c) -*Meeting The Politicians Of The German Parliament*

Although, not strictly within the scope of the Berlin program, the following brief summary of the German Federal Government's administrative setup, will be of interest to some readers.

*There are FIVE levels of administration with all delegates and functionaries within the Federal Republic being elected by the democratic process. At the lowest level, there are the LOCAL BOROUGHS and the CITY COUNCILS. In the capital, this latter function is carried out by the BERLIN SENATE which, since reunification, again has jurisdiction over both the Eastern and Western sectors of the city. The next level is taken up by the LÄNDER PARLIAMENTS, 10 of which are in the West (e.g.Baden\ Württemberg, Bavaria, North Rhineland/Westfahlen et al.), and five in the Eastern states, formerly administered by the DDR. Although, the Länder Parliaments are generally responsible for the administration of their own affairs, like the States in Australia, they are ultimately answerable to the Federal Parliament. Other parties are the Free Democratic Party (FDP), Christian Social Union (CSU), and Democratic Socialists (PDS), a 'reconstituted' Communist Party taken over from the former DDR.

Being a Democratic Government, Germany has a Federal Chancellor, (until September 2005, Herr Gerhard Schröder of the SPD Coalition with 'The Greens') and a Federal President Head of State elected to a five year office. The president appoints the chancellor, the country's chief executive official, who must then be approved by an absolute majority of the Bundestag. The president may also make recommendations for the incoming cabinet ministers, in accordance with the proposals put forward by the Chancellor at the NATIONAL level.

There are the two Houses of Parliament, the **BUNDESTAG** (Lower House of Representatives) and the **BUNDESRAT** (Upper House) Federal Council). Like the British House of Lords, the latter

---

Note:* The following information is partly based on the Microsoft Encarta© 1994 Article "Germany" by Microsoft Corporation; Copyright 1995 Funk & Wagnall's Corporation.

has the power of veto over the Bundestag. For much of the post-war period, both houses had their residence in Bonn on the Rhine, but are now again under one roof in the Reichstag Building in Berlin. Until recently, the two major parties in the Bundestag were the coalition of Social Democrats (SPD) and Green Party with the conservative Christian Democratic Union (CDU) in opposition.

Before coming to Berlin, appropriate arrangements had been made for guests interested in the political life of the capital to meet representatives and Members of the House of Representatives. Being especially interested in Germany's political and economic developments and other related issues, I had hoped that such an introduction to the City and Federal administrations would provide an insight into how some of the problems associated with Berlin's constantly changing political, social and economic environment were affecting the Jewish communities. I had also hoped for an opportunity to talk privately with a member of the Bundestag about some of the present problems facing the Parliament, such as the issue of Neo-Nazi groups. Unfortunately, this was not to be, and I was not surprised that other guests also found the 'talk-back session' with political party members somewhat impersonal and disappointing.

Note: The Federal elections held in September 2005 between the ruling SPD (Social Democrats) and the CDU (Christian Democratic Union) were so close that it took more than three weeks for the result to be finalized. The situation was made even more complicated because the ruling party also has to elect the Chancellor. Herr Gerhard Schröder, the outgoing Chancellor, representing the SPD, was being challenged by Frau Angela Merkel from the CDU. After lengthy discussions, Frau Merkel was finally elected to become Germany's first Lady Chancellor. The question of who was going to govern the Federal Republic was then settled in typically German manner, by forming a coalition between the two major opposition parties, further evidence how 60 years of democratic government have changed the heart of this nation. Where else in the world, have two major parties, representing fundamentally opposite political platforms, agreed to work together AS ONE TEAM for the benefit of the people ? The newly amalgamated major parties SPD and CDU are further supported by the Greens and other minor political parties.

There were three party representatives involved in the discussions, including the CDU (Conservative Party), SPD (Labour Party in power at that time) and the PDS (Former Communist Party). In spite of the excellent translations by the young interpreter, even with microphone and earphones, it was difficult to follow the proceedings. And then, suddenly it was all over and the guests were ushered into the next part of the program. On the whole, the visitors were left with the impression that the politicians did not really understand the concerns of Jews who had been expelled from Berlin as children and had now returned to the capital as elderly citizens for the first time in 60 years to experience for themselves Germany's new democratic parliamentary system. On the other hand, the opening address at the parliamentary session by Frau Anke Fuchs, Member of Parliament and Vice President of the German Bundestag, was more appropriate to the occasion and her comments and answers were generally well received by the guests.

THE REICHSTAG – PAST AND PRESENT

In February 1933, shortly after Hitler's accession to power, a massive fire almost destroyed the Reichstag Building. The blame was placed on Communists and Jewish collaborators, but strong evidence suggests Nazi and even US involvement

Today, The Bundestag (Lower House) and the Bundesrat (Upper House) are the landmark of the German democratic political system. The glass dome is used as a viewing platform for visitors to the proceedings.

The Reichstag-Seat Of The German Federal Parliament

T he tour of the Reichstag was of special interest to me because, as a keen viewer of the Deutsche Welle TV news broadcasts in Australia, I was eager to visit the new Bundestag Plenary Chambers, the place where Germany's leading politicians debate the country's most important issues. The first thing the visitor sees as he approaches the massive building, is the engraved inscription reminding all who enter here, that the Reichstag, erected in 1884 was dedicated by Kaiser Wilhelm II '*TO THE GERMAN PEOPLE'*. Since then, this edifice to national power, has been at the centre of German political life, first under Bismarck, then under the quasi-democratic Weimar Republic, then under the Nazi dictatorship and finally under the democratic system of the post-war Federal Republic. Older readers will recall that in February 1933, shortly before Hitler came to power, the Reichstag building was almost completely destroyed by fire. Although, it was of course politically expedient at the time to blame '*Communist and Jewish agitators'*, there is in fact considerable evidence that high ranking members of the Nazi Party were in collusion with certain foreign elements in the US to create a situation where '*The Jews'* could be presented to the masses as '*The 'REAL Enemy Of The German People'* *

After the fire in 1935, the Reichstag building was never fully restored during the Nazi era, and what remained was severely damaged by Russian shelling during the final days of WW II. Restoration work under a British architect, Sir Norman Foster, began in 1970, and over the next 29 years the massive building was restored with a totally new interior. In 1999, the new Reichstag was officially inaugurated and after their move from Bonn, is now again the official seat of both Houses of Parliament, and open to the public. Fortunately, as V.I.P.s, our group was allowed to enter the building by the West door and thereby avoid joining the long queue of tourist at the front entrance. One of the most striking features of the Reichstag is the huge *mirrored cupola* overlooking the building with its spiral walkway inside the dome. This unusual design gives a magnificent 360° panoramic view of the city and from here, the

---

Note:* *See' Wall Street And The Rise Of Hitler*
Anthony C.Sutton ; Bloomfield Books 1976.

sharp contrast between the traditional architecture in the West and the monotonous, stereotyped high-rise apartments of the former DDR, can be clearly seen. (*See Page 79*) Climbing the spiralling walkway within the dome is a most unusual experience, with the cone-shaped angled centre column made entirely of mirrors, giving a constantly distorted image of one's actual position within the dome.

THE BUNDESTAG
The House Of Representatives of The German Federal Republic

THE BUNDESRAT
Inauguration Of the Upper House September 28th. 2000

Despite Sir Norman Foster's initial reservations, he later agreed to include the dome in his design and this unusual feature is now an important tourist attraction for the thousands of visitors who come to the capital each year. Also of interest is the circular photographic display at the glass dome entrance, showing photos of the Reichstag's turbulent history born out of political intrigue, social reform, two world wars and the change from dictatorship to democracy in the post WW II Federal Republic.

The glass cupola on top
of the Reichstag Building

Panoramic view of Berlin
from inside the glass dome

Display of the Reichstag
history at the dome entrance

The never ending queue
outside the Reichstag

SOME BERLIN TOURIST ATTRACTIONS

The Federal Chancelary
Symbol of German Democracy

Checkpoint Charlie
The Museum is on the left

Frederich the Great Statue
Statesman and Philanthropist

The Siegessäule
Shadows of the past

The New Lehrter Bahnhof
Hub Of Europe's Rail Network

The Berliner Dom - Resting Place
of the Hohenzollern Dynasty

(d) -Entertainment And A Tour Of The Ancient City Of Potsdam

One of the more relaxing items on the program was the bus tour to Potsdam, a former Prussian Garrison town, some 35 Kms. from Berlin. Previously, in the Soviet occupied zone, the City of Potsdam is, since reunification, again the capital of the Federal State of Brandenburg. An interesting landmark en route to Potsdam was the **Glienicker Bridge,** an important border crossing point during the Cold War era between the American and Soviet sectors of occupation. The bridge, used by both sides for the secret exchange of espionage agents, became famous in several spy films. But above all, the City of Potsdam is renowned for its magnificent palace of **Sans Souci**, (*Fr. 'Without Care'*), built by Frederick the Great in the elegant mid 18th Century Rococo style. In this peaceful environment French was the official court language, and it was here, away from the interruptions of military life, where Frederick The Great could freely follow his philosophical and musical interests. One of the rooms in the palace is named after the Emperor's favourite visitor, the French philosopher Voltaire. Although Frederick was a military statesman, he was also highly respected for his altruistic and philanthropic principles. Typical of this philosophy, was when the palace grounds were being laid out, he decreed that a large Dutch windmill near the palace should not be moved because it was the miller's sole means of support for his family. The same windmill still stands near the palace today, testimony to a ruler who, despite his political and military power, never forgot the common man. When he died, in accordance with his philosophy, the emperor of Prussia - musician, philosopher and statesman, was buried in a simple grave in the grounds at *San Souci*, together with his favourite greyhound. The site is now a major tourist attraction.

One of the most impressive features at *Sans Souci*, are the stone steps leading to the entrance and the terraces specially designed for growing vines and fruit trees. The plants are housed in enclosed recesses, cut out of the terrace walls to protect them from winter frost. The palace and grounds were originally built on what was once a chalk quarry.

Here, the Emperor of Prussia, Frederick The Great lies buried together with his favourite hound - The simple grave of a great man.

The organised tour through this magnificent palace and grounds was a reminder of an age of grandeur long gone. Today, it is a major tourist attraction and every year, an unending queue of visitors shuffles along the corridors and stately chambers in soft felt slippers supplied at the entrance for the protection of the original timber floors.

Entrance to the Palace 'Sans Souci'

Front view of the Palace

Music Room

The 'Hanging Garden' Vines

POTSDAM

Also of interest in Potsdam were the so-called *'Russian Colony'* and the *'Dutch Quarter'* with its uniform architectural style, built in 1734 for Dutch immigrant artisans.

The Dutch Quarters at Potsdam

The final bus stop was at the **Schloss Cecilienhof** mansion just outside Potsdam, an impressive looking Tudor style mansion which became internationally famous in 1945 when on August 2nd, the so-called **"Potsdam Agreement"** was signed here by the Allied heads of state, General de Gaulle (FRANCE) Attlee (UK), Truman (USA) and Stalin (USSR). Here, the details for the partitioning of Germany after WW II were worked out which later resulted in the division of the country into four zones of occupation. The house with its beautiful gardens is now a historical memorial site open to the public.

The Cecilienhof Schloss Venue for the " Potsdam Agreement " between USA,RUSSIA, FRANCE and BRITAIN.

The Glienicker Bridge Site for the exchange of American/Soviet espionage agents

On the return trip to Berlin, we passed the new Olympic Stadium, with a seating capacity of almost 80,000 spectators, site of many pre-war political mass rallies. Older readers may remember that at the 1936 Olympics, Adolf Hitler walked out of the stadium in a rage, after Jessie Owen, the black American 'super runner' decidedly beat his German opponent. Because, under Nazi racial philosophy, blacks were regarded as *'subhuman'*, such a 'humiliation' of the German Master Race by a Negro athlete was seen by Nazi authorities as a serious 'affront' to their self-styled racial superiority.

The rebuilt Berlin Olympic Stadium

Another enjoyable event was a boat trip at the invitation of the Berlin House of Representatives - a relaxing ride on the river Spree in a very modern, luxuriously appointed boat, appropriately named *'Sans Souci'*. The trip which included an excellent buffet meal went alongside the Pergamon Museum and finished at the Berlin Cathedral. During the trip, Frau Martina Michaels, Member of the Board and Member of the House of Representatives, spoke to the guests.

As a final farewell to the capital, all participants of the program were invited to the Musical Theatre Berlin to enjoy an excellent performance of 'The Hunchback of Notre Dame', a delightful and very well performed musical with unusual stage scenery. A very enjoyable evening and a fitting farewell to an unforgettable week in "The New Berlin".

(e) - *Personal Free Time*
Dialogue with German Families

D espite the unavoidably tight schedule, the program also allowed time for the Jewish guests to pursue their personal interests such as shopping, seeing friends, or visiting their former school. Also, some guests had previously arranged to meet with German families. For those who, like myself, had chosen this option, the program generously allocated a whole Saturday. Although direct contact with a German family was seen by most participants at least as a meaningful event – perhaps, even symbolic of one's personal commitment in the reconciliation of Jews and gentiles, there were also some, who for a variety of reasons were disappointed with the experience. It was therefore not surprising that some guests were reluctant to make such a personal arrangement. I felt this was very sad and wondered if the underlying reason for such hesitance to make direct contact with German families was because they still saw such a personal involvement as an emotional barrier too hard to cross. Regrettably, even some of those who actually did meet with their German hosts were sadly disappointed. The family was either too preoccupied with various mundane tasks such as preparing for a birthday party, or were unable or even unwilling to give adequate time to what should have been for both them and the Jewish visitors an unforgettable and unique experience. And so sadly, for some guest, this once in a lifetime opportunity to establish direct German/Jewish dialogue, was lost.

I feel very strongly that such direct ***personal*** contact between ordinary German families and ex-Berlin Jews, who in many cases had come from the far corners of the Earth and had after more than 60 years returned for the first time to the City, where they had spent an often traumatic childhood, is certainly one of **_the_** most important aspects of the Reconciliation Program. My special thanks therefore go to Barbara, one of our tour guides, for arranging a visit at short notice and making this part of the program for me and my wife such a very special occasion and one of the highlights of the week. Our hosts for the day were Herr Dr.Bernd Pfeiffer, Professor at the Berlin School of Economics and his charming wife Helga who showed us some more of Berlin's great sights, invited us to share a meal with them, and in the evening took us to the Potsdamer Platz to see Berlin by night. Because we had expressed our intent to visit my former school in Berlin, they drove out to the suburb of Dahlem to find the Privatschule Kaliski in which my sister and I attended from 1938 to 1939. However, following a prolonged search, and because of the failing light, we decided to resume our quest in the morning. It later turned out that we had actually passed within a few Mtrs. of the school entrance, located in a small side street.

The brief discussions with Dr.Pfeiffer offered the first opportunity to hear the German view on some of the issues which had for so long occupied my mind. My only regret was that we could not spend more time with these very kind people. Since our visit, we regularly correspond by e-mail, and this has opened new possibilities for an ongoing exchange of ideas of mutual interest. I see the establishment of such personal relationships between individual ex–Berlin Jews and German families as one of the most important long-term benefits of the reconciliation program, not only for the Jewish guests, but also for their host families. *

Note: * *That even more than six years after our visit to Berlin, the spirit of the German/Jewish Reconciliation Program still reaches into the farthest corners of the world, is shown by the wonderful time we spent together when Dr.Pfeiffer and his wife Helga visited us in Queensland in March 2007.*

The Waldschule Kaliski -1939 and 2000

A fter our first unsuccessful attempt, my wife and I set out again the following day on our own to locate the Waldschule Kaliski in Dahlem. Incredibly, among the few things that were saved in 1939, and which survived more than 60 years of house moves in England and Australia, was the original 1938 school prospectus from which the following photos were taken. And it was this carefully preserved document, which now became our guide for locating the school.

School Front View

School Rear View
Note: Drainpipe under white arrow

Earlier enquires through the organiser of the program, had indicated that access to the school, now a residential complex and partly used by the German Archaeological Institute, would present no problem. And so, with our 1938 prospectus to hand, we entered the school grounds. Much was as I remembered it from pre-war days. As the photos on the previous page show, incredibly, even the position of the drain pipes at the rear of the building were still in evidence after 61 years. But, there were also substantial changes. What was once the outside assembly area at the rear of the building had been turned into a terraced back garden and the swimming pool, where my sister learnt to swim, had been filled in with soil. Also, there was a new building within the compound which, we were told, had been the war time private residence of the Nazi Foreign Minister Joachim von Ribbentrop.*

The Waldschule Kaliski was the last school my sister and I attended in Berlin from 1938 until our emigration to England in March 1939. As a day and boarding school, this school was regarded as one of Berlin's foremost pre-war Jewish educational establishments. Language classes were in Hebrew, German, English, French and Latin and Religious Instruction and Music formed an important part of the school syllabus. At a time of great uncertainty, when all Jewish children were threatened with expulsion from Germany, the Waldschule Kaliski, like all similar establishments, was actively training students for work in Palestine. In this regard, the school was at the forefront of this policy, and in line with other Jewish establishments, the school curriculum was essentially designed to prepare students for pioneering work in the Palestine Kibbutzim. Strong emphasis was therefore placed on student self-sufficiency and Kibbutz-like group activities formed an important part of the daily routine.

The photos page 131 show a variety of student activities in line with this policy. They are taken from the 1938 school prospectus. Many students, with or without their parents, eventually emigrated to Palestine, 'The Land Of Their Fathers ', where some, like one of my school friends, later fought and died in the 1948 War of Liberation. I still correspond by email with his brother who lives in Israel.

Note: Some readers will perhaps recall that as German ambassador, Herr von Ribbentrop signed the 1939 Soviet/German non-aggression pact with his Russian counterpart Molotov. Only months later, under 'Operation Barbarossa', German forces invaded the Soviet Union. One of his most arrogant acts however, and one for which von Ribbentrop will always be remembered, was when in 1939 as the German ambassador to England, he insulted King George VI - by giving him the Nazi salute.

STUDENT ACTIVITIES
AT THE JEWISH WALDSCHULE KALISKI
Preparing Young Pioneers For Palestine

Young Zionists training for the Kibbutz

Pioneers peeling potatoes for Palestine

STUDENT ACTIVITIES
AT THE JEWISH WALDSCHULE KALISKI
Music And Other Activities

Student participation in Music and the Arts
The Recorder Class

In the Workshop   Student Swimming Lesson

138

There was at that time a somewhat ironical situation with all Jewish schools. whose objectives were correctly seen by the Nazis as *'establishments for the preparation of Palestine pioneers'.* and since the overall policy of the Nazi government was to rid Germany of all Jews by whatever means, this Jewish strategy was 'tolerated' if not actually encouraged, in the belief that it hastened the government's own objectives. And so, until early 1939, the Nazi Education Department showed at least some tolerance because, despite totally different motives, they saw Jewish schools as 'actively working towards the same goal that is - to make Germany *'Judenrein'.*. However, in 1939, following a nationwide arrest of Jewish teachers, the Kaliski school, together with other Jewish educational establishments, was permanently closed by Nazi authorities. I remember the day we came to school, sometime after the Reichskristallnacht pogrom of November 1938, only to find most of our teachers missing. It was not until later the next day that we became aware that they had all been arrested and it was several days before they returned to school.

While walking through the school grounds, quite unexpectedly, we were joined by a middle aged gentleman. When I explained the reason for our presence he said: *"Oh, then you will be interested to see the film".* It turned out that in April 1993, just four months before our first short visit to the capital, quite unbeknown to me, a Berlin TV channel had produced a video film at a reunion of 150 former Kaliski students. Dr.Baske, a long-term resident at the school, kindly invited us to his apartment to see this video of former students relating their pre-war childhood experiences and their tales of survival in far off lands following their expulsion from the capital. Today, many of these former refugees serve their adopted countries as highly qualified professionals. The video brought back many memories of the time when the Kaliski School at Dahlem was one of the best known Jewish educational establishments in Berlin. There were more surprises when Dr. Baske produced a scrapbook with photos, newspaper articles etc. of the school's pre-war history. Finally, Frau Baske presented us with a list of all 1938 and 1939 students (including the names of my sister and myself), taken from a book **"Insel der Geborgenheit"** (Island in Seclusion). *. We thanked them for their kindness and added them to our growing list of German e-mail correspondents.

Note: * See Appendix for Publisher

The City of Berlin

Memories Of The Past And Hope For The Future

The Farewell Reception
And 'Good Bye' To The "NEW BERLIN"

T he official farewell function was again at the generous invitation of the City Senate. As the centre of the Berlin Jewish Community, the Heinrich Stahl Hall adjacent to the now rebuilt Fasanenstrasse Synagogue, was the ideal venue for reviewing the week's activities and for the organisers of the program to say *'Auf Wiedersehen'*, *'Au Revoir'*, *'Adios'* and *'Good Bye'* to all the group. In his farewell speech, Herr Michael Bruch, Acting Chief of Protocol of Berlin, stressed the outstanding success of the more than 30 year old German/Jewish Reconciliation Program which had up to then enabled more than 34,000 ex-Berlin Jews to revisit the capital and other German cities. But he also pointed out that there were still thousands of Jews in the Diaspora who had, for one reason or other, not yet availed themselves of this generous offer by the Berlin Senate.

"The Senate", he said," *had done its part, and to ensure the continuance of the program, it was now the task of those Jews returning to their homeland to encourage and persuade other Jewish ex-Berliners to share in this great experience."*

In this regard, Herr Bruch's comments were in full accord with my own sentiments regarding a **'reciprocal response'** by the partici-pants of this successful program, namely that to achieve its <u>ultimate fulfilment,</u>, this initiative needs a <u>personal commitment </u>from those who had been privileged to share this unique experience. This was the first time I heard this important issue raised in public. But, in the final analysis, the deciding factor will always be to what extent this renewed association with the German people has affected the life of individual participants, and to what extent it has motivated their desire "*to give something back in return"- to become personally involved in the program.* Notwithstanding the generally traumatic effect the Berlin experience inevitably has on all Holocaust survivors, the tearful farewell scenes outside the Hotel Berlin as the guests started to leave for home, was clear evidence that there was generally widespread appreciation for the program. As a finale and in gratitude to the many dedicated people who had made this *'once in a lifetime '* experience possible, each of the lady tour guides was presented with a large, well deserved bouquet of flowers and Herr Ruediger Nemitz, the organizer of the program, also received various tokens of appreciation. Altogether, it was indeed a sad and tearful parting -so much had happened in this memorable week - so many memories - so many impressions - so many personal experiences!

As I watched some of the guests on the last day, I wondered just what long-term impressions this visit would have on these aged ex-Berlin Jews, especially those who had lost members of their family during the years of the Holocaust - what were their thoughts as they prepared to leave, probably for the last time, the City which had so forcefully remin-

An emotional and tearful 'Good Bye' to the wonderful people who made this 'once in a lifetime' experience possible. Second on the left is Herr Rüdiger Nemitz, the program organiser.

The Author and his Wife, Sister and Husband at the Farewell Reception Dinner.

142

ded them of their traumatic childhood and the cruel murder of their loved ones? In years to come, will they be for ever haunted by the spectre of their past, or will they accept the new German reality and with enthusiasm encourage their Jewish friends back home to participate in this program ?

But as the guests made ready to leave to continue their journey elsewhere, or prepared to fly home to far off lands, there was no doubt that the majority of those who had shared this unique experience, saw the program for what it really was – an extraordinary and totally unique gesture of goodwill by the Berlin Senate, and indeed the German people as a whole towards all Jews who had as children been the victims of Nazi brutality. The words of The Mayor, Herr Eberhardt Diepgen that *"The Question of whether a person is a Jew or not, is no longer relevant in Germany today"* now took on an even greater significance and meaning. It was indeed comforting to know that most guests were leaving the capital spiritually uplifted and full of gratitude, not only for what the Berlin Senate and the Jewish communities had done for them personally, but also for what these organisations had so generously provided for thousands of other Jews in more than thirty years of the program's operation.

As for myself, I came away with a feeling of great satisfaction and gratitude, indeed humbled that I had been privileged to experience these unforgettable seven days together with my wife Stella and with my sister and her husband from England. Whereas, before coming to Berlin, I had serious doubts about Berliner's allegedly changed attitude towards the expanding Jewish population - in one week, the German/Jewish Reconciliation Program convinced me that the future welfare of Jewish communities in the capital is safe in the hands of a government and a people inspired by a new spirit of open-minded tolerance, not only towards Jews, but also towards all other minority groups in today's Federal Republic.

And so, with many memories of this week still alive, we boarded the ICE train at the Berlin Zoo station on its way South to visit a German family, who had for many years been our neighbours in Melbourne. And as the last suburbs of this great City with all its memories finally faded from view, my thoughts were especially with those Jews from all parts of the world who, for just a few days, had shared this experience with us. I felt sad that almost all would leave Berlin having merely passed '*like shadows in the night*' across my own presence in the capital. Somehow, it was difficult to comprehend that as children more than 60 years ago, we had all been victims of a common fate and that apart from this brief encounter, we would never even have been aware of each other's existence. My greatest regret is that there had been so few opportunities to become more intimately acquainted with other guests especially those from North and South America and to speak to them about their own impressions and experiences after their expulsion from Nazi Germany. Sadly, except for a very few, none of them would ever know who we were, and we would never know who they were, and so we would for ever remain just a name on the list of participating guests. And yet, I felt that although we had only spoken to a few, a *'Spiritual Bond'* had somehow been created not only with all the members of our own group and the organisers of this remarkable program, but also with the many Jews who, though unknown to us, had been earlier participants, as well as those German families who by inviting the Jewish guests to their homes, had in a sense also become important 'links' in this quest for German/Jewish friendship. The unequivocal message of this program is that effective reconciliation can only grow in an atmosphere of mutual trust and respect between individuals. In this, Germans can make no greater contribution than to seek dialogue with a former German Jew, and they in turn can show no greater personal commitment than to take that first important step *'to reach out their hand'* to the German people, thereby breaking the emotional barrier which has for generations been the cause of so much misunderstanding and distrust.

Our Hotel -The Hotel Berlin By Night

PART IV

The Enigma Of The Jews' Survival

Their Return To Germany And To The Land Of Israel

Children's choir at the 2000 inauguration of the Berlin exhibition
"JEWS IN BERLIN 1938 - 1945"

The Jews Return To Germany

F or the discerning Jewish visitor to Berlin, the evidence of the Senate's *'outstretched hand'* is not hard to find. Particularly noticeable are the street signs and buildings bearing the names of once prominent Jews, who in times past had played such influential roles in German society. Artists, such as Max Liebermann, a well-known Jewish painter of the pre-war period, Prof. Albert Einstein who in the 1930's fled to America, the 19th Century poet Heinrich Heine, the writer Thomas Mann and the composer Felix Mendelssohn, are just a few German Jews, who are today again accepted by the public without prejudice *'in their own right',* not for who they were, but for the significant contribution they made to German culture in terms of their musical, literary and scientific achievements. And, even, as this is being written, the Federal Republic is celebrating the Centenary of Prof. Albert Einstein's $E=MC^2$ publication on Relativity with its fundamentally new understanding of the laws governing Energy, Mass and Time. And this re-established 'Jewish connection' is not confined to the capital Berlin, but is evident throughout the Federal Republic. Also, in other large cities, like Frankfurt/Main, Munich and Stuttgart, with prominent pre-war Jewish populations, re-established museums and synagogues are evidence of a revitalised Jewish presence. It is also of interest that a street in the South German City of Ulm has recently been named after *'Anna Essinger,* the founder of the nearby former Jewish Landschulheim at Herrlingen, where my sister and I attended from 1936 to 1938. During WW II, the main school building was used by the German army as a rehabilitation centre, whilst a second school building became the private residence of Feldmarschall Erwin Rommel, the German commander of the Africa Korps. A bronze plaque at the entrance informs the visitor of the school's Jewish past, evidence that it is the intention of the current owners of the property to preserve the 'Jewish connection' to this building.

Such an official, pro-Jewish attitude in today's democratic Germany, contrasts sharply with pre-war days when any Jewish connection with German culture was ruthlessly suppressed. In the 1930's for instance, performances of works by Jewish artists like Felix Mendelssohn and virtuosos like Yehudi Menuhin, Jascha Heifetz, Arthur Rubinstein, to name but a few, were totally banned. The Nazis even went so far as to dismantle a statue in Stuttgart, erected by Felix Mendelssohn in honour of the composer Johann Sebastian Bach whom he greatly admired. Also the famous '***Ballad of the Lorelei'***, composed by the Jewish poet Heinrich Heine, became a target in the Nazi drive to stamp out the Jewish connection. In a feeble attempt to disassociate this popular song about the mythological *'Lorelei Rock'* on the River Rhein from its Jewish poet, the Nazi Education Ministry issued new textbooks to all State Schools describing the author simply as *'Unbekannt'* ('Unknown'). Today, Heinrich Heine's famous ballad ' *The Lorelei'*, as well as the works of all Jewish composers and artists are again recognized and accepted by the public as an important contribution to Germany's rich musical and cultural heritage.

A similar tolerance can also be found in the literary world, with no distinction being made between works by German and Jewish authors. Both are freely available to the public in libraries and bookshops and Berlin bookstalls openly display all types of specifically Jewish literary works in Hebrew and even Yiddish. Such free cultural exchange is further evidence of the cosmopolitan nature of this great city and confirmation of Herr Diepgen's statement about today's *'total integration of Jewish life into the Berlin community '*. It is also of note that Berlin newspaper articles, German books purchased during our stay in Berlin, and television documentaries based on archived German wartime material, reflect the strongest condemnation for the events relating to the Nazi Holocaust and the brutal behaviour of German forces in occupied territories during WW II. Indeed, it is an integral part of the post-war democratic freedom of expression that there is in today's Germany, the severest disapproval of *any* breech of human rights, whether directed against Jews or other minority groups. As the comments by the former Berlin Mayor show, this is especially true wherever outrages on Jewish communities occur such as the desecration of a synagogue or an attack on Jewish individuals. (*Refer P.26*) This must surely be seen as further evidence of the authorities' resolve to accept Jews in their society as citizens with equal rights.

THE JEWISH PRESENCE RETURNS TO BERLIN

The Jewish Museum

The Israeli Embassy

The Berlin Jewish Museum
Milestone In German / Jewish Relations

The Secret Of The Jew's Immortality Revealed

No account dealing with the Nazi Holocaust, can ignore the fact that the continued survival of the Jewish people in the face of such bitter and constant persecution, constitutes an extraordinary historical enigma. For centuries, Anti-Semitism in Europe with its frequent deprivation of liberty and civil rights for Jews has been a recurring threat to the nation's existence - and today, with the rise of Islamic fundamentalism, that threat to Jewish survival, is still as great as ever. Even as this page is being written, the President of Iran, Mahmoud Ahmadinejad in a speech to 3000 hardline Iranian radicals, swears " *to eradicate the State Of Israel from the face of the Earth"*, whilst the rocket attacks from fanatical Palestine terrorists on Israeli settlements, continue unabated. What then, we have to ask, is the secret of the Jew's continued survival, when powerful empires which once ruled the world, have for ever disappeared in the sands of time, or have by virtue of assimilation with their conquerors, progressively lost their national and cultural identity? Ancient Egypt, Greece, Babylon, Assyria and Rome -all are gone, yet the Jew remains and still plays a major role in the financial and artistic affairs of the world today. * Is it not a measure of their long established fiscal competence that Jews are still so prominent in the world's major economic and commercial institutions such as the World Bank, the International Monetary Fund, the US Federal Reserve Bank and many other similar organisations?

Throughout history, the excuses for persecuting the Jew have been legion. Ever since their enslavement in Egypt, more than 3000 years ago, nations have used Jewish persecution as a legitimate scapegoat to cover up their own political and territorial ambitions and failures. Under Pharaoh Ramses II (?) and the Babylonian King Nebuchadnezzar, Jews were enslaved because they were seen as a threat to the monarch's power, King Ahasuerus (Xerxes I?) of Persia set out to destroy them because they were *'different'*, the Greeks and Romans used them as slaves, the Spanish Inquisition (13th-15th Century), wreaked vengeance ontheJews for crucifying Christ and their refusal to convert to the Catholic Church.

**Note:* *Readers should be aware that the following text is in no way politically motivated, and is entirely based on historically verifiable data. All scriptural references are taken from the NKJV$^{©}$ translation of the Old and New Testaments of the Bible. $^{©}$ Thomas Nelson Inc.*

Even Martin Luther, the founder of the German Protestant Reform Movement became violently anti-Semitic when the Jews he was trying to convert to Christianity refused to give up their own faith. Jewish Persecution continued during the Renaissance in Europe. During the 17th to 19th Centuries, Jewish persecution raged unabated with pogroms in Russia and various European nations until finally, in the 20th Century, the National Socialist government in Germany, driven by a fanatical zeal to restore Arian racial purity, set out to destroy the entire European Jewish population. And yet, incredibly, despite the most cruel deprivation and suffering, the Jewish people have survived right into the 21st Century, and as the Rev.W.R.Inge, Dean of St. Paul's, London, once observed *"have time and again, stood at the gravesides of their persecutors."* As in the case of the early Christians, the inevitable consequence of persecution was dispersion into other lands, and wherever Jews settled, their skills in trading and finance soon brought prosperity to their new host country and for themselves, at least for a time, freedom from oppression.

In every country where Jews established themselves, their first priority was to build synagogues and prayer houses, the very foundation of their faith, and it was perhaps more than anything else their strict observance of dietary and religious laws, which over time, resulted in them becoming a *'separate (and despised) people amongst the nations '.*

From earliest times, Jews were particularly adept at trading and so, inevitably, when Jewish merchants and businesses prospered, rivals became jealous of their success and the riches they accrued were often seen as having been obtained by devious means and unfair trading practices. Despite the severest condemnation of such unethical dealings in their own scriptures, the sheer need to survive by any means often became the trigger for renewed hostility against Jewish communities, eventually starting another cycle of persecution in the lands of their dispersion.

Particularly Jews from Eastern Europe were frequently forced too live in isolated ghetto communities in constant fear for their lives. Set apart from the surrounding population, speaking only Hebrew and/or Yiddish, and maintaining their religious customs and traditions based on orthodox Old Testament teaching, such isolation often proved to be a 'two edged sword'. Whilst, on the one hand, ghettos created closely knit communities where the traditional Jewish lifestyle could be practiced, on the other, as shown by the events in Nazi Germany, being confined in clearly identifiable communities, also made it easy for their enemies to quickly locate and destroy them.

That, despite centuries of discrimination and constant persecution, the Jewish nation has survived to this day is, from a worldly perspective, surely one of the most perplexing historical enigmas of our time. Although, it could of course be argued that, as was the case with early Christian communities, that the survival of the Jewish people is primarily due to their dispersal into many lands, the history of other minority tribes and cultures who suffered a similar fate suggests otherwise, in that long-term assimilation with native populations, wars, deprivation and disease generally resulted in a progressive decline of culture, and eventually the demise of tribal and national identity. And, as shown in PART I, this is exactly what happened for example in Australia, where British occupation, European diseases, dispossession of native land and property, and integration under the '*Stolen Generation*' and '*White Australia*' policies, resulted in a progressive decline of native customs and practices, and in Tasmania even led to the demise of the entire Aboriginal population estimated to be approximately 2500 at that time.*

Why then, we have to ask, have the Jews survived, even into the 21st Century, when so many of the ancient civilizations have disappeared? There were in fact a number of factors which prevented the Jewish nation from following other nations into racial oblivion. Most importantly, by the time of their worldwide dispersion after the destruction of Jerusalem by the Romans in 70 AD, orthodox Judaism had already been well established in the land of Palestine for more than 500 years. Whereas a younger race would have been generally more susceptible to assimilation with their neighbours and therefore in time have been absorbed into the religious culture and practices of their host country, a spiritually less vigorous people would have lost their national identity under the ravages of persecution. In the case of the Jews, it was however more than anything, the already well established common Hebrew language of the Old Testament and the adherence of strict dieta -

---

Note: * *The last Tasmanian Aboriginal woman Truganini died in 1876 in a Hobart prison. For many years, her skeleton was exhibited in a museum, and in 1976, 100 years after her death, her remains were ceremoniously scattered over the ocean near where she and her tribe once lived.*

ry and hygienic laws and customs which, even after the nation's worldwide dispersion in AD 70, maintained a strong spiritual bond between widely dispersed Jewish communities in the Diaspora.

" *What then* ", as the writer Mark Twain once asked " *is the secret of the Jews immortality'*"? Surprisingly, the answer is that unlike other nations, the survival of the Jewish people cannot be satisfactorily explained in purely worldly terms', for the key to their indestructibility is not **WHO** they are, but *WHY* *they* are. In fact, as shown in the following pages,in contrast to any other nation, the continuation of the Jewish race as a separate people is not a secular, but a *moral* issue and can therefore not be fully explained from a purely historical point of view. Central to this fact is that, apart from the records left by Josephus, a Jewish historian from the early 1st Century AD, what we know of Judaism is largely based on the Jews' own Bible records and archaeology. When trying to find an answer to this enigma of Jewish survival, these ancient writings and the evidence they present, must therefore also be taken into consideration, for it is *only* in them, where a rational and satisfactory explanation for " *The mystery of the Jews' survival"* can be found. Fundamental to this truth is that the deliberate and ongoing separation from the nations with whom they came in contact, was not of their own choosing, but was a strict divine command to the Nation of Israel. During their long history of persecution, separation from their neighbours therefore became for Jews not only a matter of '*tribal security'*, but also an affirmation of their most basic belief -namely that they, and they alone, are *"The Chosen People Of GOD* ". And it was this mark of distinction which would ultimately become not only the reason for their continuing persecution, but also the key to their survival as a separate nation. The very raison d'être and purpose of Jewish existence throughout their long history, and indeed, in a wider sense, the rôle of Israel today as a permanent haven for Jews is enshrined in that

---

*Note: * The following quotations are taken from the NKJ (New King James) translation of the Bible. Readers may find it helpful to compare this version with their own alternative translations. The use of a Bible Dictionary and Concordance is also recommended. Please note that only the quotations which have a direct bearing on the question of the Jews' survival are cited here. To fully appreciate their relevance to the whole text, it is suggested that the remainder of the quoted chapters be read in their entirety.*

belief and forms the basis of the Zionist claim for a permanent right of occupation to the Land of Israel.

And because this perceived claim to Jewish 'Holiness' often became the trigger for persecution, it is important to understand that the nation's physical separation was also the catalyst to _enforce_ their 'spiritual separation' from the nations with whom they came in contact. Many scriptural passages, such as the following taken from the Book of Deuteronomy, speak of this special relationship the Jewish people have with their GOD.

Deut 7:6 (NKJ)

"For you are an holy people to the Lord your GOD; the Lord your GOD has chosen you to be a people for Himself, a special treasure above all the peoples on the face of the earth."

To fully appreciate this special relationship between Israel and their God, it has to be understood that the distinction of being ' **The Chosen People Of GOD** ', **was certainly not by Israel's own choice,** for it not only imposed the most stringent moral responsibilities on the individual as well as the whole nation, but also carried with it terrible retribution for non-compliance to the divine commands.

As the following quotation from the Book of Deuteronomy shows, any blessings resulting from their special status as 'The People of GOD' were to be strictly _'conditional'_ on whether they would _"diligently obey the voice of the Lord their GOD, to observe carefully all His commandments"_

Deut 28:1-2 (NKJ)

1   _"Now it shall come to pass, **if** you diligently obey the voice of the Lord your GOD, to observe carefully all His commandments which I command you today, that the Lord your GOD will set you high above all nations of the earth." 2 "And all these blessings shall come upon you and overtake you, **because** you obey the voice of the Lord your GOD"_

In this same chapter, the consequences of obedience and disobedience are clearly laid out.* It is worth noting here, that whilst only the first fourteen verses describe the blessings which would follow obedience, the remaining fifty four verses of the chapter present a list of

---

Note: * _A reading of Deuteronomy Chapter 28 is recommended_

terrifying consequences for non-compliance to the Lord's commands. The conditions spoken of in verses 53–57, have repeatedly found their prophetic fulfilment not only in biblical times, but throughout Jewish history and especially during the years of the Nazi Holocaust.

The last verse in the chapter is also interesting, for it accurately predicts the situation which followed the destruction of Jerusalem in AD 70 when, because of the large number of Jews taken in the siege, slave markets in the Middle East became so glutted that Jewish slaves sold into Egypt, were practically worthless *"and no man would buy them"*.

Incredibly, it is the Jews' own, most sacred book the Bible, which not only records the nation's consistent failure to live up to their high calling, but also vehemently condemns '*The People Of The Lord*' for their depravity and persistent defiance of His holy commands. The biblical record shows how the nation's prosperity ebbed and flowed according to their conformity to these precepts and that they became so corrupted by the religious practices of their heathen neighbours, that they even sacrificed their own children to the Canaanite god Moloch, (Heb: Molech). Taking their lead from evil minded Kings like Ahaz (*2 Kings:16 v3*) and Manasseh and, as shown by the following quotation, even King Solomon, who at first was renowned for his moral wisdom, but later built altars to pagan gods in order to placate his foreign wives, the nation of Israel slipped ever deeper into moral decadence.

I Kings 11: 7 (NKJ)

"Then did Solomon build an high place for Chemosh, the abomination of Moab, in the hill that is before Jerusalem, and for Molech, the abomination of the children of Ammon."

Jer 32:35 (NKJ)

"And they built the high places of Baal which are in the Valley of the Son of Hinnom, to cause their sons and their daughters to pass through the fire to Molech, which I did not command them, nor did it come into My mind that they should do this abomination, to cause Judah to sin."

With such a consistently damnable record, it is almost beyond belief that the Jews should still be regarded by GOD as '*His Chosen People*'. In fact, their sinful conduct went so far, that on several occasions, the Lord told Moses that He was actually thinking of destroying the entire nation for their wickedness.

Deut.9:14 (NKJ)

"Let me alone, that I may destroy them, and blot out their name from under heaven: and I will make of thee a nation mightier and greater than they."

Even when Moses relayed God's dire warning to Israel,

Deut 4:26 (NKJ)

"I call heaven and earth to witness against you this day that you will soon utterly perish from the land which you cross over the Jordan to possess; you will not prolong your days in it, but will be <u>utterly destroyed</u>."

this reproach too fell on deaf ears and, as their own records testify, GOD's people continued along their path of moral corruption and decadence.

(1) THE JEWS AS GOD'S WITNESSES

S o, why then, one has to ask, should the Jews still be so special in GOD's sight, for clearly, they have not deserved this privilege by virtue of their conduct? Part of the answer comes from the 43rd Chapter in the Prophecy of Isaiah, where it is recorded that, <u>*despite*</u> all their failings, the Jewish people were to have a unique purpose in life - for they **<u>were specifically chosen</u>** '*to be a perpetual witness to the existence and power of Almighty God.*'

Isa. 43:10-11 (NKJ)

10 *"<u>You are My witnesses,</u> "* says the Lord, "*and My servant whom I have chosen, that you may know and believe Me, and understand that I am He. Before Me there was no God formed, nor shall there be after Me. 11 I, even I, am the Lord; and beside me there is no saviour"*

In other words, the reason for the *'indestructibility'* of the Jews is that they are to be a *'visible reality', a* perpetual witness and irrefutable evidence to all nations and all ages that GOD the Creator of the universe is still in control and directs the affairs in the kingdoms of Men. (*See Daniel Ch.4 v.17*). Since, however, as we have seen, the Jewish claim to be *'The Chosen People Of The Lord'* cannot be rationalised by virtue of their obedience to God's commandments, their privileged position as GOD's Witnesses is therefore not by *'right'* but by *'**Grace***'.

In fact, so important is the Jews' role as perpetual witness to the existence of GOD, that the Lord actually stakes the functioning of the entire universe against a guarantee for the nation's survival as shown by the following quotation from the Prophet Jeremiah:

Jer 31:35-37 (NKJ)

35 *"Thus says the Lord, who gives the sun for a light by day, the ordinances of the moon and the stars for a light by night, who disturbs the sea, and its waves roar (The Lord of hosts is His name); 36 "If those ordinances depart from before Me, says the Lord, <u>then the seed of Israel shall also cease from being a nation before Me for ever.</u>"*

37 *"Thus says the Lord "If heaven above can be measured, and the foundations of the earth searched out beneath, I will also <u>cast off all the seed of Israel for all that they have done</u>, says the Lord."*

So, the covenanted relationship between God and His specially chosen people is based on , "Grace" and not 'Right'. As we shall see, this truth, constantly repeated both in the O.T. as well as the N.T. is fundamental to understanding the Gospel of Christ and therefore affects not only Jews but ALL Christians.

And overshadowing this principle is the divinely guaranteed continuance of the Jewish people ' *until the times of the Gentiles be fulfilled'*. This is brought out in the prophecy of Jeremiah, where we have the Lords guarantee that the Jewish nation, <u>because of their disobedience,</u> would be punished, but because they are to be perpetual witnesses to His existence, would never be ***totally*** destroyed – always a remnant would be saved. The following verse clearly shows who controls Israel's destiny.

Jer 30:11 (NKJ)

" _Though I make a full end of all nations where I have scattered you, yet I will not make a complete end of you. But I will correct you in justice, and will not let you go altogether unpunished._ "

<u>Note</u>: For a summary of this section - see pages 190-192

(2) THE ABRAHAMIC COVENANT

U p to now, only quotations from the Jewish Old Testament have been cited, but the New Testament, also has much to say about Jewish survival. It is therefore important to bear in mind that both Old and New Testaments are two _inseparable_ parts of the same inspired (literally 'GOD breathed') revelation, each fulfilling a complementary role in the overall purpose of GOD. This means, for a true understanding of the Christian Gospel and the apostolic letters, references to relevant Old Testament events, characters and prophecies also have to be taken into consideration. This close connection between the two Testaments already becomes evident in the very first chapter of the Gospel of Matthew, which begins with the words:

Matt 1:1 _(NKJ)_

" _The book of the genealogy of Jesus Christ, the Son of David, the Son of Abraham:_ " *

<u>Note:</u>* _According to Strong's Dictionary, the word 'Son', (Grk.. 'huios'), is a somewhat ambiguous term and may refer to the actual son of a person, a distant ancestor (as in Matthew 1:1), or even to an animal , such as a foal or young bullock._

So, right at the very beginning of the N.T., we have the proof that, the Lord Jesus Christ is a direct descendant of Abraham, the progenitor of the Jewish race, and must therefore have been a born JEW. And of course, not only Jesus, but all the Apostles including Paul, a strict Pharisee before his conversion to Christ, were Jews. Also, many of the early Christian believers were converted Jews, brought up under the Law of Moses in a traditional Jewish environment. So it is therefore not surprising that basic Christian values and beliefs also have their roots in traditional Jewish philosophy and that much of Christ's message is directly based on O.T. teaching, specifically addressed to his Jewish audience. This means that the original Gospel as taught by Jesus, must also have its roots in the Jewish O.T. and that without this fundamental background the Christian religion could not have come into being. This reality, that Christianity owes its very existence to the Jews, is now at last being recognised and accepted by an increasing number of Christian churches.

Who then, was Abraham, and what has his connection with Jesus to do with the survival of the Jews? To answer this fundamental question, we have to go right back to the record in Genesis, the first book of the Bible. In the 11th. Chapter, at the end of a long genealogy, stretching back to the sons of Noah, we read that Terah, the father of Abram[*1], lived in Ur,[*2] a Chaldean City in the Euphrates Valley, (now part of Southern Iraq), a civilisation notorious at that time for its ritual feasts involving human sacrifice to the Sumerian moon god 'SIN'. The record shows that (probably, in order to escape this evil environment), and in search of better agricultural opportunities, Terah decided to leave Ur and to settle with his family in the land of Canaan, (later Palestine), a journey of more than 1000 Kms. The route first took them to Haran (or Harran), a small town in Syria, where they settled for many years. Following the death of his brother Haran and father Terah, Abram[*], now, a wealthy

---

Note: [*1] *The son of Terah, who came out of Ur, was originally called ABRAM, a name of uncertain Semitic origin. But, following a renewal of GOD's promises, ABRAM's name was changed to ABRA(H)AM (Father of a multitude) by the addition of the Hebrew letter, 'He', (?) which signifies 'GRACE'.*

Note: [*2] *It is interesting, that there is actually a suburb in modern Baghdad, named 'UR'. However, the area occupied by this suburb today, is smaller than that of the original Sumerian City State of that name. Like other parts of the capital Baghdad, the suburb of UR has also been the target of many violent attacks by terrorists.*

man of about 75, continued his journey to Canaan, taking with him his wife Sarah, his nephew Lot and servants.

In Genesis, Chapter 12, we read of an extraordinary dialogue between GOD and Abram which was to form the basis for all God's future relationship with mankind.

Gen 12:1-5 (NKJ)

1 *"Now the Lord had said to Abram: "Get out of your country, from your family and from your father's house, to a land that I will show you."*

2 *"I will make you a great nation; I will bless you and make your name great; and you shall be a blessing."*

3 *"I will bless those who bless you, and I will curse him who curses   you; <u>and in you, all the families of the earth shall be blessed</u>."*

Following a strife between the herdsmen of Abram and those of his nephew Lot, the Lord again spoke to Abram, this time extending the promises to include the land of Canaan (Palestine) <u>for an everlasting possession</u>. Similar promises are later repeated to Abram's son Isaac and his grandson Jacob.*

Gen 13:14-17 (NKJ)

14 *And the Lord said to Abram, after Lot had separated from him: "Lift your eyes now and look from the place where you are- northward, southward, eastward, and westward; 15 for all the land which you see   <u>I give to you and your descendants forever</u>".*

16 *"And I will make your descendants as the dust of the earth; so that if a man could number the dust of the earth, then your descendants also could be numbered." 17 "Arise, walk in the land through its length and its width, <u>for I give it to you</u>."*

Whilst, it is on these GOD given promises to their forefathers that today's Jews base their claim for 'rightful possession' of 'ERETZ ISRAEL', the Land of Israel, * it is the consistent refusal of the Palestinians and other Arab countries even to admit Israel's right to exist, which has, since 1948, been the primary cause for continuing hostilities between the Jewish State and her neighbours.

The theme of these promises is taken up in the N.T. where, in the 11th Chapter of Hebrews, the writer emphasizes that Abram's journey to Canaan (now, the Land of Israel), was an act of extreme FAITH in the promises GOD had made to him.

Heb. Ch.11:8 (NKJ)

" *By faith Abraham obeyed when he was called to go out to the place which he would receive as an inheritance. And he went out, not knowing where he was going.* "

Now, Abraham was 99 years old, and his wife Sarah had been unable to produce an heir. Abraham's second wife Hagar, a bondwoman therefore bore their first-born son Ishmael, who later became the progenitor of the Arab nations. Events soon took a dramatic turn, when during another encounter with an angel, Abraham was informed of the forthcoming miraculous birth of a son by Sarah. And it was through this second son Isaac, not through Ishmael the firstborn, that the Abrahamic covenant as recorded in Genesis Chapter 12, was to be continued to all coming generations, for God had said:

Gen 17:18 (NKJ)

"I will establish my covenant with him for an everlasting covenant and with his descendants after him". *"For in Isaac shall your seed be called"*. **Gen. 24:12 (NKJ)**

But Abraham's greatest test of faith concerning Isaac, the seed of promise, was yet to come. We read of this in Chapter 22.

Note 22: * Following an encounter with an angel of the Lord, Jacob's name was changed, to 'Israel', (Heb: ' A Prince with GOD '), and throughout the O.T.,the Jews are referred to as ' The Children Of Israel '.

It should also be noted that the word 'Angel ' in Scripture merely denotes a 'heavenly messenger'. It is recorded that both Abraham and Jacob at first see their heavenly extra-terrestrial visitor as a 'Man'. This verifies many other accounts in the Bible where God's messengers are not at first recognized as such, because they appear in human form.

Gen:1-2 (NKJ)

1 " *Now it came to pass after these things that God tested Abraham, and said to him,"Abraham!".And he said," Here I am." 2 And He said, "Take now your son, your <u>only </u>son Isaac, <u>whom you love, </u>and go to the land of Moria, and offer him there as a burnt offering on one of the mountains of which I shall tell you."*

9 *Then they came to the place of which God had told him. And Abraham built an altar there and placed the wood in order; and he bound Isaac his son and laid him on the altar, upon the wood.. 10 And Abraham stretched out his hand and took the knife to slay his son.*

11 *But the Angel of the Lord called to him from heaven and said, "Abraham, Abraham!" And he said, "Here I am." 12 and He said, "Do not lay your hand on the lad, or do anything to him; for now I know that you fear God, <u>since you have not withheld your son, your only son, from Me.</u>"* (See Note next page)*

Gen 22:15-18 (NKJ)

15 *Then the Angel of the Lord called to Abraham a second time out of heaven and said: "By Myself I have sworn, says the Lord, because you have done this thing, and have not withheld your son, your <u>only </u>son;*

17 *"Blessing I will bless you, and in multiplying I will multiply your descendants as the stars of the heaven and as the sand which is on the seashore; and your descendants shall possess the gate of their enemies. 18 "In your <u>seed </u>all the nations of the earth shall be blessed, <u>because you have obeyed My voice.</u>"*

There is an important New Testament reference to this event, where in Chapter 3 of his **Letter To The Galatians**, the Apostle Paul points out that the word '**seed**' in verse 17 above, is not in the plural , but in the <u>singular,</u> which he says, refers to Christ. In other words, **CHRIST IS THE SEED PROMISED TO ABRAHAM** in whom all the nations of the earth are to be blessed. This confirms Matthew's Gospel Ch.1:1.record that Christ is a direct descendant from Abraham to whom the promises were first made.

Gal. 3:16 (NKJ)

*Now to Abraham and his Seed were the promises made. He does not say, "And to seeds," as of many, **but as of one,** "And to your Seed," **who is Christ.**"*

Time and again, these promises made to the '(fore)fathers', are given as the principal reason for GOD's continuing relationship with the Nation of Israel, but also, as the above quotations show, they form an important link between the Old and New Testaments.

Perhaps, the most important aspect of Abraham's test of faith is the connection between his ready compliance to sacrifice his son Isaac and the promises concerning '*the promised Seed,* the Lord Jesus Christ. How strong was that faith ? Did he firmly believe that *had* he actually slain Isaac, the only heir to the divine covenant, **GOD would be true to His word, and would raise him from the dead ?** The writer to the Hebrews (Generally accepted to be the Apostle Paul) in Ch,11 v.17-19 alludes to this incident confirming Abraham's supreme faith and its significance.

Hebr. 11: 17-19 (NKJV)

*17 "By faith Abraham, when he was tried, offered up Isaac: and he that had received the promises offered up **his only begotten son,** 18 Of whom it was said, That in Isaac shall thy seed be called: 19 Accounting that God was able to raise him up, even from the dead; from whence also he received him in a figure"*

We have here a symbolic image of Christ's own death and resurrection and a typical example of what in scriptural terms is called **A Type Of Christ'**

Note: * *It should be noted that at that time there was no divine law forbidding this evil practice. Having spent his childhood in the moon worshipping City of Ur and now living in Canaan, Abraham knew that the ritual offering of children to their gods was an accepted heathen practice and regarded by their society as ' the ultimate sacrifice '. GOD's specific command for Abraham to sacrifice his own beloved son Isaac, in whom the promises were to be fulfilled, was therefore not only the patriarch's ultimate sacrifice, but also the supreme test of his faith in the divine promises and his GOD.*

In John's Gospel Chapter 3 v.16, one of the best known verses in the New Testament, GOD reiterates Abraham's willingness to sacrifice his beloved son Isaac by allowing His only son Jesus to die on the cross.

John 3:16 (*NKJ*)

*"For God so loved the world that **He gave His only begotten Son** that whoever believes in Him should not perish but have everlasting life."*

Again, as it was for Israel, this promise to the Christian believer was also to be **CONDITIONAL,** requiring from the potential disciple *first*, a true understanding of the promises made to Abraham , *then* a 'sealing' of the believers' relationship with his/her new master by total immersion in the waters of baptism, and *finally* a life-long commitment to live in accordance with the commandments of Christ.

It is interesting at this point to look at the origin and meaning of Christian baptism which is derived from the Greek word 'baptizo', a term used in the textile dying industry to describe the act of totally immersing a fabric material into a dye, in order to change the colour of the entire garment. Whilst the practice of baptizing by total immersion was the only form of baptism known in NT times, (even Jesus was totally immersed in the river Jordan) (See also Acts Ch.8:38/39), the practice of sprinkling only the head of infants was not introduced by the Church until much later in the Christian era. Most importantly, however, the Apostle Paul in his letter to the Romans Chapter 6, points out that total immersion in water is not only symbolic of the baptismal candidate's death' to his/her former lifestyle', but also, the public affirmation required prior to immersion and the subsequent 'rising out of the waters' constitutes for the responsible adult believer a personal lifelong commitment *'to walk in newness of life'* that is, according to the commandments of Christ. It is this important analogy, clearly brought out in Paul's letter to the Romans Chapter 6* which is absent in the infant christening ceremony as practiced by many churches.

Also, as the following selected verses from Paul's Letter to the Galatians Chapter 3 show, the believer's new relationship with Christ, whether Jew or Gentile, calls for a mandatory submission in the waters of baptism.

Gal 3:6 -9 (*NKJ*)

6 *"Just as Abraham believed God, and it was accounted to him
for righteousness. 7 Therefore know that <u>only those who are
of faith</u>, are sons of Abraham."*8 *"And   the   Scripture,
foreseeing that God would justify the Gentiles by faith,
<u>preached the gospel to Abraham beforehand</u>, saying, "In you
all the nations shall be blessed". 9 So then those <u>who are of
faith</u> -are blessed with believing Abraham."*

The same chapter concludes with this dramatic statement:

27 " *For as many of you <u>as were baptized into Christ have put on
Christ</u>." 28 "There is neither Jew nor Greek, there is neither
slave nor free, there is neither male nor female; <u>for you are
all one in Christ Jesus</u>. 29 <u>And if you are Christ's, then you
are Abraham's seed, and heirs according to the promise</u>."*

It should also be noted that because the Abrahamic covenant is
<u>exclusive</u> to those Gentiles <u>and</u> Jews who have been baptized 'into
Christ', the widely held belief among Christians regarding 'universal
salvation', therefore lacks scriptural support.

*<u>Note</u>: * A reading of this chapter is recommended.*

Mount Moriah, where God's
promises were made to Abraham

(3) THE RETURN OF THE JEWS TO THE LAND OF ISRAEL

W e now come to the third and most important reason for the Jews' survival into the 21st Century. We have already seen that because, as the Prophet Isaiah states – *"they would not walk in GOD's ways, neither were they obedient to His laws"*, the Jewish people were to be scattered into all the countries of the world. Although, much of the Old Testament refers to Israel's earlier history and scattering among the nations, the biblical record also accurately predicts their eventual return in ' *the latter days* 'to the land of Israel promised by GOD to Abraham, Isaac and Jacob as an everlasting possession. And it is in the continuing existence of the State of Israel against all odds, even into the 21st Century, that the survival of the Jewish people takes on its greatest significance in our own time.

Many Bible passages, such as the following, predict the eventual return of the Jews to their ancient home land Israel:

Jer 30:3 (NKJ)

"For behold, the days are coming,' says the Lord, that I will bring back from captivity My people Israel and Judah,' says the Lord. 'And I will cause them to return to the land that I gave to their fathers, and they shall possess it."

Jer 16:15 (NKJ)

" But, 'The Lord lives who brought up the children of Israel from the land of the north and from all the lands where He had driven them.-For I will bring them back into their land which I gave to their fathers."

The return of the Jews to the Land of Israel first became reality at the end of the 19th Century, mainly due to the courage and vision of two men,–Dr.Theodor Herzl, (1860-1904),a Hungarian born Jewish writer / journalist and founder of the Zionist movement, a quasi-political organi -

Note:# The following information is partly based on the article 'Israel (Country)'© Microsoft Encarta® Encyclopaedia 2005 Microsoft Corporation 1993-2004. All rights reserved sation devoted to tne *'Jews for Palestine'* concept, and Dr.Chaim Weizmann, (1874-1952), a Russian born chemical engineer living in England, who later became Israel's first president,

Much of the momentum for the new movement came at that time from a pamphlet *'Der Judenstaat'* (The Jewish State), published in 1896, in which Dr.Herzl called for an *internationally recognised homeland* for all Jews in Palestine. He saw such worldwide acceptance of the Jewish claim for a permanent national home in Palestine as an essential preliminary requirement for the establishment of a future sovereign State of Israel. It-is interesting, that exactly, as so dramatically described in Ch.37 of Ezekiel's prophecy, Jewish immigration began *as a small trickle of migrants* from Eastern Europe at the end of the 19th Century. In 1897, with Dr.Herzl as president, the first Zionist Organisation convened in Basel, Switzerland, to officially proclaim Palestine as the site for the future Jewish State. The newly created World Zionist Congress was to provide economic and financial support.

Throughout the next decades, under the strong leadership of Dr.Chaim Weizmann, the Zionist movement continued to grow. During WWI, as director of the British Admiralty Laboratories, Dr.Weizmann had been responsible for the discovery and development of synthesizing propanone (acetone), an important component in the manufacture of explosives. When the British government sought to recognise this major contribution to the war effort, Dr.Weizmann, deeply committed to the Zionist cause, refused any personal recognition, but forcefully presented his case to the government for a permanent Jewish home in Palestine. The British response was an ambiguously worded document which became known as *"The Balfour Declaration of 1917"*. Whilst, on the one hand, this expressed support for the establishment of a permanent Jewish home in Palestine, it also stated: *"That it was to be clearly understood that nothing shall be done which would prejudice the civil and religious rights of existing non-Jewish communities in Palestine, or the rights and political status enjoyed by Jews in any other country"*.

Although the *"The Balfour Declaration"* was in reality no more than a letter from Lord Balfour, the British Foreign Secretary to Lord Rothschild, a powerful Jewish financier, this ostensibly altruistic document nevertheless had an immediate and profound effect on Jewish political claims to the land of Palestine. But this letter also revealed a 'hidden', less benevolent British government motive - namely her real

WWI military objectives in the Middle East. In 1917, with Palestine still under Turkish Ottoman rule, it was vital for Britain to have the support of both Jews and Arabs. The Balfour Declaration with its ambiguous bilateral undertaking to appease both sides, was therefore largely directed towards soliciting both Jewish and Arab support for the war effort. Whilst, on the one hand, it was especially important for Britain to gain the financial support of Jews in the United States with their strong influence on world money markets, it was equally expedient for Britain to placate the Arab Chieftains who controlled the pipelines carrying Middle East Oil to the Mediterranean terminus at Haifa. In the long term, however, Britain's Middle East policy was principally determined by the geographical position of Palestine, a strategically important country at the cross roads between Europe, Asia and Africa with excellent harbour facilities at Haifa on the sea route to India. Furthermore, the establishment of a Zionist State under British mandate protection would give Great Britain military and economic possession and control of this important region. On July 24, 1922, *"The Balfour Declaration"* was embodied in the League of Nations' mandate for Palestine, which set out the terms under which Great Britain was entrusted with the temporary administration of the country on behalf of its Jewish and Arab inhabitants. And in May 1948, following the total withdrawal of all British troops from Palestine, 31 years after its original proclamation, the establishment of a national home for Jews in Palestine as outlined in *"The Balfour Declaration"*, became the basis for the newly consecrated independent State of Israel. Dr. Chaim Weizmann became the nation's first president.

Ever since its inception, this controversial document has been regarded by both Arabs and Jews as legally binding, committing the British government to support their respective claims for a national home in Palestine and there is little doubt that the ambiguous commitments to both sides as outlined in the 1917 *"Balfour Declaration"*, have been a contributing factor in the continuing political struggle between the State of Israel and the Palestinians.

Whilst during the early 20th Century, Jewish immigration into Palestine continued at a steady rate, in the pre-war period, under the threat of Nazi persecution, immigration rose dramatically. Out of an estimated German/Jewish population of 525,000 living in Germany at that time, 280,000 emigrated worldwide of which 150,000 Jews from Germany,

Austria and Eastern European countries were able to escape to begin a new life in Palestine. Most of those who were unable to save themselves, were later deported and murdered in one of Hitler's death camps.

Following the liberation of Auschwitz and other Nazi concentration camps in 1945, many Holocaust survivors with the help of the Red Cross and Jewish relief organisations made a determined effort to enter Palestine legally. However, tough British immigration laws and a naval blockade off Haifa and other ports, made legal immigration virtually impossible. Many Jews therefore had no choice but to resort to illegal means of entry - a desperate decision which cost many their lives. Nothing however, could stop the flood of Jewish refugees determined to enter Palestine - neither the blockade of British warships, nor even the forced deportation of 1750 illegal immigrants to the island of Mauritius and Madagascar in the Indian Ocean. Most, had not only endured the horrors of the Nazi death camps, but in many cases, were now the only members left of their murdered families. Knowing that resettlement in the Land promised to Abraham *as an everlasting possession'* was their last and only chance of survival, the determination of these survivors from Hitler's death camps to be part of the new State of Israel, knew no bounds.

To understand what happened next, one has to consider the dilemma faced by the British at that time. As the occupying power, they had not only to maintain law and order in their mandated Palestine territory, but also had the difficult task of restricting the immigration of Jewish settlers whilst placating local Arab chieftains who controlled Middle East oil. Although some Jews during WWII, taking enormous risks, had managed to get to Palestine illegally, on the whole, the strictly enforced immigration quota of 75,000 which had been set for the duration of the British mandate, had up to 1945 prevented an overwhelming influx of Jews into Palestine. This, however, was about to change for, in the light of the immediate post-war release of tens of thousands of Jewish survivors from Nazi concentration camps, determined to enter Eretz Israel by any means, the British were forced to reconsider their Palestine policy. This led to a special session of Parliament where orders were issued to the navy that Jewish illegal immigration into Palestine was to be stopped ***at all costs***. The entrances to Haifa harbour and other ports were to be blocked and all Jewish immigrants were to be transferred to other ships for transport back to European ports, if necessary by brute force.

In accordance with the new ruling, all ships coming from Europe to Palestine with illegal Jewish refugees were now intercepted by the British navy and prevented from entering Palestine territorial waters by whatever means the navy chose. This often resulted in ships being deliberately rammed in international waters or otherwise disabled to make them incapable of moving. Any resistance by the Jews was to be met with tear gas grenades, guns and rifle butts. Ships were boarded by naval commandos and all passengers were transferred to other vessels, often with great brutality against women and children and forcibly taken back to their European embarkation port or as in some cases, to the islands of Madagascar and Mauritius in the Indian Ocean.

Clearly, Britain no longer really knew what to do with these thousands of survivors from Hitler's death camps. Their only thought was now ' *to get rid of them* ' and make some other country responsible. As more and more ships tried to break the British blockade, even the world media turned against these desperate Holocaust survivors, portraying them as '_the_ *'cause', rather than the victims of all that trouble in the Middle East*".

How soon the world had forgotten the graphic pictures of battle hardened British and American soldiers in tears, when only two years before, they had liberated the German death camps and witnessed the emaciated, living skeletons of Jewish survivors! But, as far as the British were concerned - in 1947, the oil treasures of Arabia were clearly of greater importance than the lives of so many troublesome Jews.

However one tries to justify the insensitive attitude of the British government at the time, such unwarranted action by the navy to attack and board unarmed foreign ships in international waters, was by any standard, a blatant violation of maritime law. Such unmitigated brutality against these desperate refugees seems all the harder to comprehend, when it is recalled that it was the British government who in 1938 and 1939, in an unprecedented act of compassion, had opened their country to almost 12,000 Jewish refugee children (including this author) and allowed them to come to England under the 'Kindertransport' rescue scheme.

No incident during this tragic period better expresses the fanatical resolve of these survivors from Hitler's death camps to enter the 'Promised Land', than the heroic action by Yossi Harel, the young Jewish commander of the ship '*Exodus*'. A well documented film of the same name graphically describes his desperate attempt to break the naval blockade of British warships outside Haifa harbour in 1947. His heroic action to turn world opinion in the Jews' favour, has not only become a symbol for the Jewish right to emigrate unhindered to Israel, but also an emblem of hope for all the world's oppressed, still under the yoke of foreign domination.

Originally an obsolete American ferry boat, the *'President Warfield'*, renamed the *'Exodus 1947'*, (later *'Exodus'*), had been purchased by the Jewish Haganah Organisation for the sole purpose of transporting illegal immigrant Holocaust survivors to Palestine. On July 11th 1947, the *'Exodus'* left the port of Séte ,near Marseilles with 4515 Jewish immigrants snatched from Europe's over-crowded post-war displaced persons camps. They had finally made it to Séte, thanks to the incredible efforts by the Aliyah-Beth rescue organisation and other Israeli underground movements, who against almost super-human odds had organised train and shipping transports from various secret departure ports in Eastern Europe.   And so, under the watchful eye of a British naval flotilla, these survivors from Hitler's death camps, including 655 children of all ages and a brigade of the Haganah Palmach Commandos began their fateful journey to *'The Promised Land'*. Sadly, despite all efforts, some of these refugees perished on the journey before reaching Eretz Israel.

THE 'EXODUS'

Note : *The following information is partly based on the book* *"Commander of the Exodus" by Yoram Kaniuk;* © *Grove Press, New York 1999*

\# After leaving France, the *'Exodus'* continued its hazardous journey along the Egyptian coast to El-Arish, before turning North towards Palestine. On July 18th, one week after the ship had left France, the British navy put into operation its well rehearsed battle plan to prevent at all costs, the *'Exodus'* from entering Haifa harbour. This was to be the 'test case' to prove to the world that British naval power was not only victorious at sea, but could even prevail against a few thousand desperate Jewish Holocaust survivors, determined to start a new life in Eretz Israel. And so, while still in international waters near the Palestine coast, this severely overcrowded, barely seaworthy vessel of only 1800 Tonnes with more than 4500 Jewish refugees on board was viciously attacked by British naval ships. The assault began with a concerted effort by five warships to repeatedly ram the *'Exodus'* simultaneously, resulting in severe, but not fatal damage to the ship. Finally, forced to stop, British naval commandos stormed aboard the *'Exodus'*, using tear gas grenades and rifle butts against the unarmed Jews trapped below deck. During the ensuing skirmish, three refugees died and thirty were wounded, as they tried desperately to defend themselves against the invaders with sticks and tin cans. It seems particularly sad to think that these long-suffering Jewish refugees, when almost in sight of the *'Promised Land'*, should now become the victims of British brutality, when only two years earlier, British troops had saved them from the horrors of the Nazi concentration camps, where many members of their families had been murdered.

Despite serious damage to their ship, the spirit of the Jews who, for the first time in their lives had actually sighted the *'Promised Land'* remained undaunted. But, in the end, the odds were against this brave little ship and her Jewish passengers and crew. Following her cruel encounter with the naval destroyers, the severe damage to the hull was beginning to take its toll on the steering and handling of the vessel.

During a short lull in the fighting, a British Dr. from one of the destroyers attended to the wounded whilst the 'Exodus' slowly continued her journey towards the port of Haifa. Finally, after every effort to gain legal entrance into Haifa harbour had been rejected by the British High Commissioner, the *'Exodus'*, still under naval escort, was ceremoniously towed into the harbour.

Nothing can describe this 'victory of the human spirit over adversity' better than the following extract from the back cover of the book " *THE COMMANDER OF THE EXODUS*", already alluded to earlier. *(See next page)* .As a fitting recognition of the triumphant entry of the 'Exodus' into Haifa harbour this event has been immortalized in the deeply moving music of the film 'Exodus'.

But, this was no ordinary home coming. For these Jews, who had already suffered so much, who had escaped from the horrors of the Nazi death camps and survived the horrendous journey from Eastern Europe to France, just to set foot, if only for a brief moment, on the land promised to their forefathers Abraham, Isaac and Jacob, was the most un-forgettable experience of their lives.

> *"The State of Israel was not established on May 15th 1948 when the official declaration was made at the Tel Aviv Museum. It was born nearly a year earlier on July 18th 1947, when a battered and stricken American ship called 'President Warfield' whose name was changed to 'Exodus', entered the port of Haifa with its loudspeakers blaring the strains of the 'Hatikvah'. The State of Israel came into existence before it acquired a name, when its gates were locked to Jews, when the British fought against the survivors of the Holocaust. It came into existence when its shores were blockaded against those for whom the State was eventually designated."*
>
> *"Commander of the Exodus"*   *Jossie Harel*
>   *Yoram Kaniuk*

However, the fight for survival for these 4515 Jewish men, women and children, was far from over and the future now looked even grimmer than ever. The British High Commissioner determined to enforce the uncompromising new regulations, now prepared the next frightening ordeal for these already severely traumatised Jews. As soon as the *'Exodus'* tied up at Haifa harbour, British armed commandos, again using tear gas, forced the Jews to transfer to other ships for return to a French port. Heavily outnumbered, the refugees fought back with whatever means were available. But, after such a long period of deprivation and so shortly after their horrendous ordeal with the British navy, before long they had to give up the struggle and all passengers were forcibly transferred to other ships. Again they were faced with the terrible journey back to France and an unknown future. After one week, they arrived at Port-le Bouc, where French authorities refused to force them to disembark, but instead offered them unrestricted free passage into France. Only a few, however, including the sick, accepted the French offer, whilst the majority refused to leave their ship, except to disembark in Eretz Israel.

The situation for these poor survivors now looked grim indeed and there was no indication from the authorities just how long they were to remain in France, or what the British planned to do next. Were they to be left simply to rot in the ship without ever realizing their only hope to start a new life in Eretz Israel? Nobody could foresee how long they would be able to survive under these appalling conditions. With temperatures in the ships rising above 40°C and in anticipation of a long siege, food was rationed, sanitary facilities were drastically overhauled and medical provisions were organized. Worst of all, was the overcrowding. In order to get as many people on board as possible, the maximum space which could be allocated to each person was an area less than 1 SM. For the next 24 days, in conditions which must have brought these survivors to the limit of human endurance, with food strictly rationed, unbearable heat below deck and every resource stretched to the limit, they waited, not knowing what their fate would be.

With nowhere to go and conditions on board for the refugees becoming more critical by the hour, the British were already secretly making preparations for the next, and in many ways, the Jews' most terrible ordeal. On August 22nd, the refugee ships again left France and made their way to Hamburg in the British Zone of occupation. Here, armed troops again forced these wretched survivors to disembark before transporting them to detention camps near the ancient Baltic town of Lubeck. One of these camps was the former Nazi concentration camp at Poppendorf. In fact, the British authorities were so insensitive to the feelings of these death camp survivors that they put them in with other prisoners, some of whom had been on the staff of former German concentration camps.

When the ships finally arrived in Hamburg, it was already dark and the ship commander requested that in order to recuperate from their long journey, his *'passengers'* be allowed to remain on board until morning. This was granted and enabled the disembarkation to take place in daylight under the watchful eye of the German and foreign media who, on seeing the pitiful condition of the refugees, most vehemently condemned this cruel action by the British as a blatant violation of international law and the British government as uncaring and even criminal. And most importantly, unlike previous media reaction, the world press and radio now recognized the Jewish refugees as the *'victims'*, not as the cause of their own misery.

Overnight, the decision to take these Jews back to Germany where many had already suffered so much, had become a major British P.R. disaster. This was especially embarrassing for the military administrations who, were at that time desperately keen to promote an image of British moral superiority and 'fair play' to the German population.

Although, many Jews were eventually able to emigrate to the USA, South America and elsewhere, after the declaration of the State of Israel in 1948, a substantial number of migrants managed to make their own way to the Promised Land. Sadly, during the time of the British mandate, many illegal immigrants perished in their attempt to enter the country either en route or, as in the case of the ship *'Patria',* even at the very gates of Haifa harbour.

As mentioned earlier, in a 1940 White Paper, the Palestine High Commissioner had set a quota limit of 75,000 Jewish immigrants for the duration of occupation, mainly aimed at placating Arab chieftains and ensuring British access to Middle East oil facilities during and after the war. Most significantly, to further solicit Arab support, the clause in the Balfour Declaration, pledging Britain's assistance in the establishment of a National home for Jews in Palestine, was now withdrawn.

* In November 1940, at a time when Britain was fighting for her very survival in Europe and on the high seas, Italy had allied herself with Nazi Germany, and Italian submarines became a constant threat to British shipping in the Mediterranean. Yet, despite the enormous risks, 2000 Jewish refugees from Eastern Europe attempted the impossible and

---

'Note: * *The following information is partly based on an article by Eva Feld, "Holocaust Survivors Try To enter Palestine – The Story Of The SS Patria "available from website:*
http://www.jewishmag.com/46mag/patria/patria.htm

boarded two small barely seaworthy ships, the *'Milus'* and the *'Pacific'* in a Rumanian port in a desperate attempt to somehow reach *'The Promised Land'*. But sadly, their efforts proved futile. With the Palestine blockade in full force, both ships were immediately intercepted by British warships on entering the Mediterranean from the Black Sea and forced to continue their journey to Haifa under the watchful eye of a powerful naval task force. However, because these ships were too small and structurally unsuitable for the transportation of illegal Jewish migrants to the Island of Mauritius in the Indian Ocean, a larger, more robust ship,the 12,000 Tonne S/S *'Patria'*, later renamed *'Molodet'* (Hebr.*'Homeland'*), awaiting repairs outside Haifa harbour, was chosen for the task. She was just one of several vessels commandeered at that time by the British navy to transport illegal Jewish refugees back to Europe or to the Indian Islands of Mauritius and Madagascar.* This draconian measure was ostensibly justified by Palestine authorities because of an alleged Zionist plot to use illegal immigration as a 'front' to infiltrate Jewish anti-British spies into the country. Every legal effort by the Jewish Committee to stop the *'Patria'* from departing Haifa failed and the British High Commissioner remained adamant to enforce his ruling on transportation of illegal immigrants.

On hearing that the 1500 Jews transferred from the *'Milus'* and the *'Pacific'* to the *'Patria'*, were earmarked for transportation to Madagascar, and that they would not even be allowed to return to Palestine after the war, the refugees made the grim decision that they would rather perish in sight of the Promised Land than endure yet another journey into oblivion. Though they were not yet aware of it, in only a few days, for many on board, this would become a terrible reality. With every legal avenue to stop the ship from sailing now exhausted, the Jewish Committee and other officials realised their options were fast running out. It was therefore in sheer desperation that the decision was then made to do something more drastic to delay departure of the *'Patria' in* order to gain extra time for negotiations with the British authorities. The initial plan was to damage the *'Patria'* just enough to prolong the time she would have to be in Haifa harbour for mechanical repairs. The main consideration would however have to be the safety of those on board. To this end, a small explosive charge was to be laid on the outside hull at the rear of the ship, away from the passengers. However, because of the difficulty in actually laying the charge with the

British navy patrolling the harbour, this proved impractical and so an alternative, more drastic method was considered. Also, because it was certain that the British would eventually board the *'Patria'*, arrangements had been made for as many Jews as possible to jump off the ship immediately before the arrival of the boarding party. The bomb was to be primed to ensure adequate time for the Jews to jump overboard

Thus, if everything went according to plan, by the time the bomb exploded, most of the passengers would have been safely picked up by surrounding ships. The first attempt to detonate the bomb failed, but on November 25th , a second bomb hidden in a sandwich tin and packed neatly between sandwiches and a thermos flask, was set to go off at a time when British troops would be searching the inside of the ship. However, the plan to cause only minimal damage went terribly wrong and the bomb exploded prematurely, ripping a huge hole in the hull, causing the 12,000 Tonne *'Patria'* to keel over and sink in less than 15 minutes.

Many on board, including some British soldiers, died in the explosion. To make the situation even worse, in the ensuing panic, a British officer accidentally shut a security door, thereby closing off any escape for many of the Jews on board. Some were able to be rescued from the sea as they hung desperately onto the sinking hull of the ship. Despite a massive rescue operation by British soldiers and naval personnel, Palestine Police, Jewish and Arab harbour workers, at least 180 refugees died in the disaster and an estimated 267 passengers were missing. While, some Jews were able to swim to shore, many more were rescued in small boats. Others took advantage of the turmoil and disappeared somewhere in the City of Haifa and surrounding districts. All those caught by the British were taken to the Atlith detention camp to await transportation to Mauritius.

Even after this disaster, the British High Commissioner still refused to cancel the deportation order and it was the British government, fearing another P.R.fiasco, who finally relented. In the light of mounting adverse world opinion, it was decided that '*as a special dispensation of*

Note: *It is indeed ironic that it was also Madagascar which had been earmarked by the Nazis as a potential home for Jews expelled from Germany. The island is notorious for its severe climatic conditions.*

mercy', and in view of the tragedy, the survivors of the *'Patria'* would not now be deported to Germany or France but all illegal Jewish immigrants would in future be sent to detention camps in Cyprus.

The early withdrawal of British troops from Palestine and the establishment of the State of Israel was now only a question of time. At the end of 1947, no longer able to control the situation, Britain had had enough, and at last conceded that Jewish illegal immigration could not be stopped. Shortly after turning the problem over to the United Nations, all British troops were withdrawn from Palestine. In an unanimous vote by the Security Council and a majority vote in the General Assembly on the future of the country, the resolution to divide Palestine into separate Jewish and Arab States was adopted. It was the first, and in many ways the most far reaching unanimous decision ever undertaken by the United Nations Security Council. Furthermore, the unprovoked attack by the British navy on ships carrying unarmed Jewish refugees was declared a blatant breach of international maritime law. It seemed, at last the world was beginning to regard the plight of Jewish refugees not as a local, but as a world problem. The Jews, seeing such a changed attitude, as the fulfilment of their ancient prophecies, were overjoyed by this new development and wholeheartedly accepted the UN plan for partition. And in May 1948, after nearly 2,000 years of persecution, worldwide dispersion and untold hardship, the first Prime Minister, David Ben Gurion proclaimed the new *State of Israel.*

As was to be expected, the decision to establish a permanent home for Jews in Palestine was received with outrage by the Arab camp. Within 24 hours, troops from Jordan, Egypt, Syria, Lebanon and Iraq assisted by Arab forces from within Israel, attacked the fledgling State. As the world watched in unbeelief, the newly formed Israeli Defence Force (IDF), outnumbered 7:1, soundly defeated the Arab invaders.

It is interesting here to recall an extract from a book *"Elpis Israel"*, (The Hope Of Israel), written **in 1848**, by a medical practitioner and devoted Bible student, Dr. John Thomas. Basing his reasoning entirely on Bible prophecy at a time when Palestine was still part of the Ottoman Empire, and Russia was ruled by the Tsar, he accurately predicted these inevitable events *one hundred years before the inauguration of the State of Israel:*

"But to what part of the world shall we look for a power whose interests will make it willing, as it is able, to plant the ensign of civilization upon the mountains of Israel ? I know not whether the men, who at present contrive the foreign policy of Britain, entertain the idea of assuming the sovereignty of the Holy Land and of promoting its colonization by the Jews; their present intentions however, are of no importance one way or the other, because they will be compelled by events soon to happen, to do what, under existing circumstances Heaven and Earth combined could not move them to attempt. The finger of GOD has indicated a course to be pursued by Britain which cannot be evaded and which her counselors will not only be willing , but eager to adopt when the crisis comes upon them. "

(Elpis Israel -14th Edition Page 442)

As GOD's promises to Abraham were being dramatically fulfilled before the eyes of the world, how many who lived through these momentous times, or were even eye witnesses of these events, recognised in them *"The Revealed Hand of the Lord"* as foretold by the ancient Jewish prophets ?

Here was the visible evidence that just as the Bible had predicted, despite centuries of bitter persecution and worldwide dispersion, a remnant of ' *His Chosen People'* was again standing at the gates of *'The Promised Land'.*

Ezekiel 6:8; 36:24 (NKJ)

8 "*Yet I will leave a remnant, so that you may have some who escape the sword among the nations, when you are scattered through the countries. 24 For I will take you from among the nations, gather you out of all countries, and bring you into your own land.*"

Again, it should be noted that as the following verse shows, the return to the *'Promised Land'* was *not* as a reward for the nation's obedience to GOD's Laws, *but that His Name might be glorified.*

Ezekiel 36:22,23 (NKJ)

22 *"Therefore say to the house of Israel, 'Thus says the Lord GOD: "I do not do this for your sake, O house of Israel, but for My holy name's sake, which you have profaned among the nations wherever you went. 23 "And I will sanctify My great name, which has been profaned among the nations, which you have profaned in their midst; and the nations shall know that I am the Lord," says the Lord GOD, "when I am hallowed in you before their eyes"*

The Flag of Israel – Witness to the fulfilment of GOD's promises

-·-·-·-·-·-·-

So far, it has been shown that to answer the question: **"What Is The Secret Of The Jew's Immortality'**, the following **three** factors have to be taken into consideration – namely:

1. Their divinely appointed role as '**Witnesses to the existence and power of GOD'** which imposed upon all Jews a strict moral code of conduct as 'His Chosen People'.

2. **Their direct descendency from Abraham, Isaac and Jacob,** to whom the original divine promises were made.

3. **The return of the Jews to Israel in the latter days**, to the land GOD had promised to Abraham 'for an everlasting possession', **not by right, but by GRACE**.

In the following sections, we shall look at five more aspects of

"What Is The Secret Of The Jew's Immortality" ?

181

The Restored Kingdom
The Significance of the Land
The Future King
The Future Status of Jerusalem
The Constitutional Laws

-.-.-.-.-.-.-

(4) THE RESTORED KINGDOM OF ISRAEL
CENTRE OF FUTURE WORLD GOVERNMENT

There is an even more important reason why, despite unrelenting persecution and their never ending struggle to remain a separate people among the Gentiles, the Jews *had* to survive to our own time. For, it is in what the Bible calls ' *The Latter Days',* they are destined to fulfil their most important role in the Ultimate Purpose of GOD.

So, what is that Purpose and what does the Jews' own Bible actually have to say regarding this? Again, we find the N.T. in perfect scriptural harmony with the O.T. On one occasion when, because of their consistent disobedience, the Lord had threatened to utterly destroy his own people, their leader Moses pleads for them in a desperate attempt to stave off the destruction of Israel as a nation. And the Lord hears and makes this profound statement:

Num 14:20-21 (NKJ)

Then the Lord said: "I have pardoned, according to your word; 21 *"but as truly, as I live,* **all** **the earth shall be filled with the glory of the Lord."**

And, looking forward to that time, Habakkuk, one of the Minor Prophets, reiterates the same theme.

Hab 2:14 (NKJ)

"For the earth will be filled with the knowledge of the glory of theLord, as the waters cover the sea"

Here, we have a preview of a '*New World Order'*, not based on human greed and military power, but on the righteous Laws of GOD. As we shall see, this is in fact the same '*New World Order'* referred to by

Jesus in many of His parables and also by the Apostles. as '*The Kingdom Of God*', or '*The Kingdom Of Heaven*'.* Christ's teaching about 'The Kingdom of God which He is to re-establish and rule over on Earth when He returns (At His Second Coming), is one of the most fundamental and most misunderstood themes in the NT. Because Christ's teaching so compellingly supports the O.T.,appreciating the significance of this association, is also crucial for understanding not only the reality, but also the *purpose* of the Jews' survival.

Here are two of the many N.T.passages which either refer directly or allude to 'The Gospel of The Coming Kingdom of God on Earth'.

Mark 1:14 (NKJ)

Now after that John was put in prison, Jesus came into Galilee, preaching the gospel of the Kingdom Of GOD"

Acts 19:8 (NKJ)

And he (Paul) went into the synagogue and spoke boldly for three months, reasoning and persuading concerning the things of the Kingdom Of GOD"

To understand the special place which the Land of Israel and the Jewish people will have in this New World Order, we have to go back in time and look at the conditions which prevailed in Palestine at the beginning of the 1st Century. At that time, the land was under the cruel yoke of Roman occupation, dominating the political, religious and social life of the nation. And when the Jews saw the occupying troops marching through the streets of Jerusalem, they remembered that 1000 years before, under King David and Solomon, *their* nation had been one of the greatest kingdoms on Earth. But, this ancient Kingdom of Israel was no ordinary kingdom, for by GOD's own decree, it was called **"The. King - dom Of The Lord"**. (See I Chron. Ch 28 v.5). In other words, this was a kingdom where the **LAND**, the **PEOPLE**, the **KING**, the **CAPITAL CITY** and the **LAWS** were all expressly chosen and set up by GOD. And, as the 'Chosen People of the Lord, it was the Jews who were given

---

Note: * *It should be pointed out here that the widely held belief that this 'Kingdom' is **in** Heaven, has **no** scriptural validity. The gospel writers consistently only speak of Christ's future kingdom as being ON EARTH. This is in accord with the promise made to Abraham (See Genesis Chs. 13,v.14,15)*

183

the awesome moral responsibility to be the custodians of that kingdom. However, because of the nation's ongoing apostasy and corruption, after King Solomon, **"The Kingdom Of The Lord"** was split into two, the Northern Kingdom of Israel and the Southern Kingdom of Judah. Whilst Israel, went into Assyrian captivity under Shalmaneser V (727-722 BC), the southern kingdom Judah continued until the late 6th Century BC, when it fell under Babylonian domination. After the destruction of Jerusalem by King Nebuchadnezzar in 586 BC and the Babylonian captivity, both kingdoms practically ceased to exist.. Although, there was some revival first, under Nehemiah (5th. Century BC) and later under Judas Machabeus (164 BC), for almost 1900 years after the destruction of Jerusalem by the Romans in AD 70, only a handful of Jews remained in Palestine. Since then, there has <u>never</u> been another Kingdom of Israel and no King has ruled over the nation.

Is it any wonder then, that when the Jews saw the miracles Jesus performed, they asked Him: "Will *you at this time restore the kingdom to Israel"?* Here was a man who could heal the sick, make the blind to see, the deaf to hear, feed the hungry, still the storm, and even raise the dead to life. And so, they wondered: *"Was this the long awaited Messiah who would save the people from Roman oppression and restore the Nation of Israel to its former glory ?"*

But when the Jewish elders realised that Jesus was not in fact their expected warrior king, and that He had no intention of overthrowing the Roman oppressor, they vehemently turned against Him and finally handed Him over to Pilate to be crucified with the accusation that Christ's claim to kingship was a direct challenge to the authority of Caesar. Since that time, the Jews' rejection of their Messiah, with the cry :*"We Have No King But Caesar !",* has echoed down the Centuries as the ultimate indictment of the nation.

So, when Jesus was speaking to the Jews in parables about the Kingdom of GOD, was He in fact referring to a physical restoration of the ancient Kingdom of Israel? Surprisingly, the answer is both *'YES'* and *'NO'*, because, although the State of Israel inaugurated in 1948, is eventually destined to become the administrative centre of the Lord's re-established ancient Kingdom of Israel, as we have seen from a previous quotation, this kingdom will extend far beyond the present borders of Israel – for it is to be a <u>worldwide</u> empire where *"<u>all</u> the earth will be filled with the glory of the Lord."*

It is also important to understand that whilst this kingdom will in many ways be totally different from any other form of human administration, like any earthly kingdom, besides the general population, it will also be made up of the four basic elements listed below. As we shall now see, each of these elements has a direct connection to the future role of the Jewish people as 'God's Witnesses', and hence their survival as a nation into the 21st Century. The four elements are :

      a) The Land,
      b) King
      c) The Capital City
      d) The Constitutional Laws

-.-.-.-.-.-.-

(a) THE LAND

It has already been shown that the Land of Israel was promised by GOD to Abraham and his descendants as an everlasting possession and that the future Kingdom of GOD will in fact be the restored ancient Kingdom of Israel. But what about Israel's actual physical location on the Earth's surface? What is so special about the tiny State of Israel that it should have been chosen by the Lord to be the centre of His future worldwide Kingdom? Taking into consideration the size of the country, a mere 22,000 Square Kms, and an overall population of just over 6.1 Million, (2005) - from a worldly point of view, there seems little reason for this choice but, as we shall see, Israel has a number of unique features which make it in fact _the_ most appropriate place on Earth for a worldwide administration. Perhaps most significant is that **_Israel is exactly at the centre of the Earth's maximum geographical land mass_**. It is also interesting that the associated militarily implications of this did not escape the Emperor Napoleon, for when asked where he would place the administrative centre of his expanding empire, he answered without hesitation: **_"Jerusalem, for THIS is the centre of the world"._**

Readers can check Israel's unique geographical position for themselves with a free standing globe. Because approximately 75 % of the Earth's surface is covered by water, when the globe is turned around its axis, much of the visible land mass will be surrounded by large amounts of ocean, until there comes a point where the land mass exceeds the oceanic area. This occurs only in <u>one</u> position, and that is _when Israel_ *is at the centre.* (*See Map below*). In this position, the map encompasses the largest populated area, encompassing the whole of the **European, African** and **Asian** continents, - including **China** and **India,** the two most populous nations with a combined population of over 2 Billion people, and the Northern part of **Canada**. The only other large land mass not covered is South America, most of Australia and the sparsely populated Pacific region. The map therefore covers a land mass representing approximately 5.6 Billion people, or nearly 96 % of the present TOTAL world population.

ERETZ ISRAEL – THE CENTRE OF FUTURE WORLD GOVERNMEMNT
The World Map With Israel At The Centre

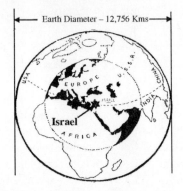

Now further consider Israel's unique position in the world:

- *It has both a temperate and tropical climate.*

- *It has both Western and Eastern sea outlets*

- *It lies at the historical and cultural intersection of three continents Europe, Asia and Africa.*

- *It lies at the centre of the world's population areas.*

- *It is at the centre of three of the world's great religious movements, Judaism, Christianity and Islam.*

- *From here, the Christian Gospel went out into all the world*

- *Here, Jesus was born, lived, died and ascended to Heaven and from here he will return to rule His worldwide empire from Jerusalem.*

- *Here will be fought the final battle of Armageddon*

(b) THE KING

A kingdom requires a king. In the past, many ambitious and ruthless kings have tried to be '*Masters Of The World*' and failed. Although ancient empires such as Babylon, Assyria, Persia, Greece, Rome and the Chinese succeeded in conquering what to them was '*the then known world*', other parts of the Earth not yet discovered, such as North America, South America and Australasia, remained largely unaffected. Neither could the kings of Spain, Holland or Portugal in the 15th to 18th Centuries, Napoleon in the 19th Century, or the German Nazi government in the 20th Century with its self-styled '*Thousand Year Reich*', or even the British Empire which in its heyday covered more than 1/5 of the earth's surface, achieve <u>total</u> world domination.

When we look at our present world with its fiercely competitive economic rivalry between nations, the problem of finding a universally accepted ruler becomes even more complex. Even, if such a person could be found, would the United Nations give him/her a universal mandate to stamp out the worldwide, extremely lucrative armament industry and thereby put at risk the employment of millions of workers in many member countries? Would such a leader be able to control large multi-national corporations engaged in the production of nuclear and toxic chemical weapons of mass destruction? How would he/she deal with the ever growing problem of river and ocean pollution? Would he/she have the power to restrain political and religious fanatics and <u>*force*</u> all nations to teach their children the art of peaceful coexistence? And most importantly, would such a world leader have total control over the world's banking system and international markets?

When we think about this seriously, look at today's fierce competition between nations, vying for an ever greater share of the world's available resources, and consider the many conflicting vested interests in the United Nations dictated by expediency, prestige and national status, it becomes self evident that from a human point of view, there is simply no way such a person would be either capable of such a momentous task, or be <u>universally</u> accepted. The question therefore remains: *Where can such a leader be found, a man or woman capable of <u>permanently</u> ruling the world in peace, free from corruption and hatred – **a role model for all nations ?***

187

To answer this complex and controversial question, we must again turn to the historical record of the Bible. In the 21st Chapter of Ezekiel's prophecy, it is recorded that in 586 BC, the Babylonian king Nebuchadnezzar II besieged Jerusalem and made Zedekiah, who had no legal right to the throne, ruler over the Southern kingdom of Judah. But, like most of Judah's kings, " *He did what was evil in the sight of the Lord.*"   In a fierce condemnation of the nation's and the king's own wickedness, the prophet Ezekiel therefore pronounces the end of the Kingdom of Judah, the tribe from which the promised Messiah was to come.

Ezek 21:25-27 (NKJ)

25 " *Now to you, O profane, wicked prince of Israel, whose day has come, whose iniquity shall end,* " 26 *Thus says the Lord GOD: Remove the turban, and take off the crown; nothing shall remain the same. Exalt the humble, and humble the exalted* " 27 "*Overthrown, overthrown, I will make it overthrown! It shall be no longer, <u>until He comes whose right it is, and I will give it to Him</u>* "

This prophecy brings out two important points. Firstly, that after its destruction by King Nebuchadnezzar, the Kingdom of Judah was to be restored at some unspecified time in the future with a king who, unlike Zedekiah, would be the ***rightful*** heir to the throne of Judah (and Israel), and secondly, that the restoration of the Israelite kingdom at that time would not be theirs by ' ***Grace*** ' - a ' **Gift from GOD** ' to the new king. ("*I will give it to Him*")*. Understanding this is important, for the Bible repeatedly states that ***<u>GOD alone is the rightful owner of the Land of Israel</u>*** and that the nation of Israel was merely appointed to be its protector and guardian. This means therefore that irrespective of any political or historical justification, from a <u>scriptural perspective</u>, the Zionist claim for '*rightful*' possession of Eretz Israel cannot be sustained. In fact, as the following passage from the Prophecy of Ezekiel shows, the Lord strongly condemned the Jews' performance as custodians of the land and it was largely this failure which eventually led to their expulsion and worldwide dispersion.

<u>Note:</u>* *Readers may recall that GOD's covenant with ABRAM regarding possession of the Land of Israel was 'sealed' by a change to his name from ABRAM to ABRA<u>H</u>AM, by the addition of the 5th Hebrew letter 'He' (?) which signifies 'Grace'.*

Jer.2:7 *(KJV)*

"And I brought you into a bountiful country, to eat the fruit and its goodness; but when ye entered, you defiled **my land**, *and made* **my heritage** *an abomination"*

Many other Bible passages in both the O.T. (*e.g. Psalm 72*) and the N.T. (*e.g. Matth: 2:2*) refer to this future Jewish King ' *whose right it is'*. Perhaps, the most important reference is found in the Second Book of Samuel where in Chapter 7, King David is given a 'preview 'of the coming MESSIAH King and his Kingdom.

2 Sam 7:12-13 *(NKJ)*

"When your days are fulfilled and you rest with your fathers, I will set up your seed after you, who will come from your body. and I will establish the throne of **His** *kingdom forever."*

The suggestion is sometimes made that this prophecy actually refers to Solomon, David's own son, (*who came from his body*). Such an interpretation however, does not satisfy the other criteria, as both the kingdoms of Israel and Judah progressively declined after King Solomon's reign and eventually, after the Babylonian conquest, ceased to exist altogether. Since the prophecy clearly speaks of a kingdom which was to last *'forever'*, this passage can only refer to the coming Kingdom of GOD when Christ will reign from Jerusalem as the rightful heir to the re-established throne of Israel and Judah.

The Jewish leaders frequently challenged the Lord's authority. Although they generally regarded Him as *'The son of Joseph the carpenter'*, it is recorded that on numerous occasions during His ministry Jesus was referred to by the people as *'The Son (Descendent) of David."* When therefore Jesus asked *"What think ye of Christ - whose son is He?*, they answered: *'The Son Of David'*. This is significant because, if the Jews believed Jesus was the legitimate 'Son' (descendent) of King David', they must also have known from the scriptures quoted above of GOD's promise regarding **the one whose royal throne would be established for ever.**

Remarkably, this promise to King David concerning *'The Rightful King'*, who was destined to restore the Kingdom of Israel, was already made 1000 years before the birth of Jesus, and was precisely fulfilled over twenty eight *consecutive* generations, (*See Matthew 1:17*).   Not only does the royal line from King David to Christ go through His earthly father Joseph, but *also* through His mother Mary.   Readers with a mathematical aptitude may like to calculate the probability of such a dual event occurring over twenty eight *consecutive* generations. The promise to King David also confirms many other passages that the Kingdom spoken of here will be *'an everlasting kingdom'*. And, when we turn to the NT, we find that even before Christ's birth in Bethlehem   (which is called the 'City Of David), the promises made to King David 1000 years before, are repeated to His mother Mary, as recorded in the Gospel of Luke:

Luke 1:31-33 *(NKJ)*

31   *"And behold, you will conceive in your womb and bring forth a Son, and shall call His name Jesus. 32 "He will be great, and will be called the Son of the Highest; and the Lord God will give Him the throne of His father David." 33 "And He will reign over the house of Jacob forever, and of His kingdom there will be no end."*

News of the birth of a Messiah King was even 'written in the heavens'. Notwithstanding, the many explanations for 'The Star of Bethlehem', (the latest research even suggests this unusual event was due to the emergence of the planet Jupiter behind the moon coinciding exactly with the time calculated by the Magi), there is much evidence that indeed *'something'* extraordinary was expected to occur precisely at that time in 'the land of the Jews'. It is interesting to speculate to what extent the decision to undertake such long journey after observing *'the sign'* was influenced by their knowledge of the Jewish scriptures, wherein more than 700 years earlier, the prophet Micah had accurately foretold the birth of the Jewish Messiah King in Bethlehem of Judea, (*Micah Ch5:2*).   Again, in what is termed *'the 70 weeks prophecy'*, Daniel ,the Jewish Master of the Magi at the Babylonian court of King Nebuchadnezzar, had predicted the exact time of the Messiah's birth (*DanielCh9:25*).   Whatever 'the sign' was which the Magi had seen in the East, it must have been sufficiently important for them to undertake a journey', probably from Persia, over hundreds of Kms. of inhospitable and often dangerous country, for no other reason than to find *'The King of the Jews'*.   Matthew's gospel (*Ch2:1-6*) records the Magi's urgent quest to find the Christ child *in **Bethlehem** as prophesied by Micah *'that they might worship Him'*, a clear sign of their recognizing the infant as a king.

Matt 2:1-2 (NKJ)

Now after Jesus was born in Bethlehem of Judea in the days of Herod the king, behold, wise men from the East came to Jerusalem 2, saying, "Where is He who has been born King of the Jews? For we have seen His star in the East and have come to worship Him."

Also, the, precious gifts they brought - Gold, Frankincense and Myrrh are again highly significant in that they foreshadow Christ's special attributes among men – namely **Gold - '*His Royal Title,* Frankinsense- '** *His Divine Character'* and **Myrrh - '** *Symbol of His Death and Burial in the Tomb.'*

But when 30 years later Jesus began His ministry, the Jewish leaders were not looking for a 'gentle' Messiah, but a warrior king who would deliver the nation from the yoke of Roman oppression. However, this is not what they found - for here was a man who by His almost mesmerising ability to control the people, was fast becoming a threat to their own authority - a man who could make the blind to see, the deaf to hear, the lame to walk and even raise the dead to life - a man who astonished his hearers, for He taught them not as the scribes, but as one *'having (divine) authority'*.

Little wonder then that the leaders of Israel, seeing Jesus as a threat to their privileged position and driven by envy and jealousy, sought how they might destroy Him. But the Pharisees feared the people's reaction and under Roman rule were not allowed to carry out the death penalty themselves, except by stoning, as specified in their law. Being unable to find creditable witnesses, the Jewish leaders therefore hastily convened a mock trial in the night, before handing Jesus over to the Roman governor Pontius Pilate with the accusation that Christ's claim to be a king was a potential threat to the Roman Emperor Caesar. And from that time, the Jews' declaration: *"We have no other king but Caesar",* has echoed down the ages as the nation's final rejection of their Messiah.

When Pilate, unable to find any cause worthy of death in the prisoner asks Jesus: *"Are You the King of the Jews?",* Jesus answers: *"It is as you say." But my kingdom is not of this world, else would my servants fight".* Jesus was telling Pilate that His claim to kingship was in fact <u>no</u> threat to the Emperor and that the Jews' accusation was false. At that point, having found no crime worthy of death in his prisoner, the

191

governor would have released Him, but the Jews cried out, saying, *"If you let this Man go, you are not Caesar's friend. Whoever makes himself a king speaks against Caesar"* .And so, Pilate now seeing his own authority being challenged, symbolically *'washes his hands of the innocent prisoner's blood'* and orders Jesus, the King of the Jews, to be taken to Calvary- there to be crucified.

Perhaps the most powerful evidence for Christ's claim to kingship, however, comes in fact not from His own statement to be a 'KING', but from Pontius Pilate the Roman governor who had placed an inscription over the cross, in Greek, Latin and Hebrew: *'This is Jesus of Nazareth -the King of the Jews'.* When the Pharisees asked Pilate to change this statement to *"He said He was the King of the Jews"*, Pilate refused, thus confirming not only Christ's rightful claim to kingship, but also that by his orders to crucify Jesus, **both** Jews **and** Gentiles (he and the Roman soldiers under his command) were consenting participants in the death of the Jewish Messiah King.

(c) THE CAPITAL CITY JERUSALEM

A kingdom without a seat of government, is a kingdom without authority. From here, the king rules – it is the centre of his administrative power. In this regard, Jerusalem is **UNIQUE**, for of no other city has GOD declared:

2 Chr 6:6 (NKJ)

*"But I have chosen Jerusalem, that **My** name might be there; and have chosen David to be over **My** people Israel".*

Both O.T. & N.T. passages refer to Jerusalem's unique status. In Matthew's gospel, Jerusalem is spoken of as *"The City of the Great King"* and the prophet Jeremiah refers to it as *" The Throne of the Lord",* other passages in the OT confirm that this ancient City which was already Israel's capital at the time of David and Solomon, is to become *'The Chosen Capital Of God's Future Kingdom'.*

Jer 3:17 (NKJ)

"At that time they shall call Jerusalem the <u>throne of the Lord</u>; and all the nations shall be gathered unto it, to the name of the Lord, to Jerusalem: neither shall they walk any more after the imagination of their evil heart."

Jerusalem is also historically significant because of its association with two important biblical events – Abraham's intended sacrifice of his son Isaac on Mount Moriah, one of the hills surrounding the city, and the fact that Israel's King David, reigned for 33 years from here over the "Kingdom of the Lord."

The City of Jerusalem played a most important rôle in the life of Jesus. Here, He spent much of His ministry, was crucified, rose from the dead, ascended into Heaven and will return again. The Book of Acts, Chapter1 records the promise associated with this unique future event. As the speechless disciples watched in awe their Master being taken up into heaven, they are told by an angel that this was to be the exact manner in which Christ was to return.

Acts 1:9-12 (NKJ)

Now when He had spoken these things, while they watched, He was taken up, and a cloud received Him out of their sight. 10 And while they looked steadfastly toward heaven as He went up, behold, two men stood by them in white apparel, 11Who also said, "Men of Galilee, why do you stand gazing up into heaven? This same Jesus, who was taken up from you into heaven." shall so <u>come in like manner</u> as ye have seen him go into heaven". 12 Then they returned to Jerusalem from <u>the mount called Olivet, which is near Jerusalem,</u> a Sabbath day's journey.

Again, we see here the perfect harmony between the Old and New Testaments, for in the Prophecy of Zechariah, written more than 500 years earlier; it is recorded that the Messiah would return to the Mount of Olives outside Jerusalem, the exact spot from which He was taken up.

Zech 14:3 (NKJ)

"And in that day His feet will stand on <u>the Mount of Olives,</u> which faces Jerusalem on the east. And the Mount of Olives shall be split in two, from east to west, making a very large valley; half of the mountain shall move toward the north and half of it toward the south".

The record shows that the return of Christ to the Earth will trigger a massive earthquake in the local geological fault line causing the Mediterranean Sea to extend right up to Jerusalem thereby making the city a major port and changing the physical topography of the entire Middle East region.

Zech 14:8 _(NKJ)_

*"And in that day it shall be that <u>living waters</u> shall flow from Jerusalem, half of them toward the eastern sea and half of them toward the western sea; in both summer and winter it shall occur".**

<u>Note:</u> * Some scholars (e.g. Matthew Henry et al) interpret 'living waters' in this verse as referring to "Spiritual Waters", in line with the NT teaching of Jesus, suggesting a spreading of " The Waters of Life', i.e the Gospel message into the far corners of the earth. However, since the word 'living' is also translated elsewhere as 'strong', and verse 3 speaks of the <u>physical</u> splitting of the Mount of Olives, it seems therefore more likely that v.8 also refers to an actual geographical event that is a massive earthquake rather than a spiritual symbolism. Since the whole of this area is at the centre of a major geological fault line, running roughly North /South through the Land of Israel, such a catastrophe could occur at any time in the future.

The Mount of Olives where Jesus
was taken up into Heaven

(d) THE LAWS

E very responsible government has to have a legally binding constitution and laws to ensure the well-being and prosperity of its citizens. In the ancient Kingdom of Israel, and throughout the long history of Israel's dispersion., the Jewish Law, essentially based on the ten commandments given to Moses and the 'People of the Lord' at Mount Sinai, established the moral fabric of the nation*. This written law, collectively known as the *'Torah'*, forms the basis for the spiritual and physical constitution of the Jewish nation and is according to Judaic belief *"The 'Revealed Word Of God To His Chosen People".* It imposes on every Jew and Jewish society as a whole, a mandatory sense of moral responsibility towards their GOD and all members of the community. The Torah Law also played an important rôle in forging a common bond between widely separated Jewish communities in exile. From earliest times, it became the focus of Jewish worship, exerting a strong stabilizing influence on all its adherents. Their unshakable belief that they were 'special' - the *'Chosen People of GOD"*, helped Jewish communities to survive throughout their long history of persecution and dispersion. In addition to the *Torah*, since the beginning of the 1st. Century AD, the *'Mishnah'*, a verbal interpretation of the Law, and the *'Talmud',* with its rabbinical expositions, have been the principal means for orthodox Jews to study the Law.

Although, the coming Kingdom of GOD will in some ways be like any 'earthly' kingdom, the laws governing the population, will not be drawn up by a human legal system, <u>but will be written in the hearts and minds of its citizens.</u>

Ezek 36:26 -28 (NKJ)

"A new heart also will I give you, and a new spirit will I put within you: and I will take away the stony heart out of your flesh, and I will give you an heart of flesh. 27 "I will put My Spirit within you and cause you to walk in My statutes, and you will keep My judgments and do them."

<u>Note</u>: * Even today, the judicial systems and social ethics of almost every civilized country are based on at least some aspects of the Ten Commandments. "Thou Shalt Not Kill", "Thou Shalt Not Steal", "Thou Shalt Not Bear False Witness" are just as legally and morally binding in the 21st. Century as they were 4000 years ago for the Children of Israel.

In his letter to the Galatians, the Apostle Paul gives some important guidelines regarding morally acceptable human behaviour and shows that aggressiveness, greed, hatred, jealousy and pride etc. which inevitably lead to the destabilization of human societies, are contrary to true Christian conduct and teaching and will have no place in the coming Kingdom of GOD.

Gal 5:19-21 *(NKJ)*

"Now the works of the flesh are evident, which are: adultery, fornication, uncleanness, lewdness, idolatry, sorcery, hatred, contentions, jealousies, outbursts of wrath, selfish ambitions, dissensions, heresies, envy, murders, drunkenness, revelries, and the like; of which I tell you beforehand, just as I also told you in time past, that those who practice such things will not inherit the Kingdom of God."

The Apostle then sets such negative, anti social misconduct against those virtues which build up and edify human relationships and which form the basis of true Christian commitment.

Gal 5:22 (NKJ)

"But the fruit of the Spirit is love, joy, peace, kindness, goodness, faithfulness, gentleness, self-control longsuffering. Against such there is no law."

Again, in his letter to the Colossians, the Apostle Paul gives this more specific advice:

Col. 3:19-23 (NKJ)

19 **Husbands** - *love your wives and do not be bitter toward them.*

20 **Children** - *obey your parents in all things, for this is well pleasing to the Lord.*

21 **Fathers** - *do not provoke your children, lest they become discouraged.*

23 **Masters** - *give your bondservants (workers) what is just and fair.*

" Repay no one evil for evil. Have regard for good things in the sight of all men. 18 If it is possible, live peaceably with all men. Do not be overcome by evil, but overcome evil with good". (Selection from Romans. Chapter 12)

Despite the relentless media glorification of war and justification of every evil under the sun, there is little doubt that it is nevertheless mankind's greatest hope one day to live in peace and harmony with one another in a world no longer threatened by wars and famine. Many Bible passages such as this prophecy of Isaiah, look forward to an age when under the authority of Christ, this dream will be realised..

(*See also Psalm 72*)

Isa 2:4 (NKJ)

"He shall judge between the nations, and rebuke many people; they shall beat their swords into ploughshares, and their spears into pruning hooks; <u>nation shall not lift up sword against nation, neither shall they learn war anymore</u>".

However, before there can be universal peace, there has to be a ***radical change in human nature*** based on a more compassionate attitude towards other people and cultures, and a deeper understanding of Man's relationship with and dependence on the natural environment. Most importantly, there has to be a <u>spiritual</u> transformation, a reappraisal in mankind's understanding of how the historically diverse values of different races, religions and nationalities can make valuable contributions to the overall welfare of the human race as a whole. It is these barriers which now divide peoples and nations - the causes of wars, poverty, and the moral breakdown of society. Where religious bigotry, political expediency, economic greed and corruption are regarded as legitimate means to exploit poorer nations, universal peace, social justice and equity cannot exist.

It would however surely be over-optimistic to expect that such a change of heart would originate in a fiercely competitive market environment, where the wealth and resources of this world are largely controlled by governments in cohort with a few powerful financial interests. Because of this inequity such an economically driven system creates, the decision making process is today generally more concerned with profitability and 'saving face' politically, than with finding solutions. Global decisions, especially those affecting climate change, may therefore have serious long-term consequences. And it is precisely because governments for political expediency and economic reasons so often show themselves reluctant to act in time, that increasingly, natural and man-made disasters like Chernobyl (Inadequate maintenance), the Sumatra Tsunami (Procrastination over a Pacific early warning system) or the Rwanda massacre (Delay in UNO assistance) occur. History shows that such major catastrophes are invariably linked to economic considerations. The warning signs are clear - with every decade, our world is slowly but surely heading towards a climax - and the Earth is now fighting back!

Alarmed by continuing exploitation of natural resources, not only religious leaders, but scientists have for years been warning governments of the long-term consequences of illegal rain forest destruction, rampant industrial and automotive pollution, and over-exploitation of the oceans. Some experts even predict that for this present generation, time is running out and that unless urgent worldwide action is taken, especially with regard to world climate change, some parts of the Earth will soon no longer be able to recover from the damage inflicted by Man. The loss of over ¼ Million lives in the 2005 Indonesian Tsunami the global increase in hurricane and bush fire activity, rising ocean temperatures and sea levels in the Pacific region, escalating earthquake, volcanic and landslide activity, massive <u>simultaneous</u> floods in opposite sides of the globe, the shifting monsoon causing unpredictable weather patterns, increasing temperatures in Greenland and the Polar regions, worldwide epidemics such as AIDS, Ebola virus, bird flue etc, super bugs and an ever increasing population - all these are nature's warnings that our planet is in serious distress. And not only governments and large corporations are to blame, but it is all of us, especially in the West, who as unintentionally wasteful consumers, living in an affluent throw-away society, are indirectly responsible for what is happening to our planet. *And despite all the evidence, there are still those with vested interests who deny the harmful effects of global warming mainly brought about by a worldwide increase in industrialisation and consumerism.*

Everything therefore points to the reality that before there can be universal peace, *the priorities of Mankind will have to change! As long as* the destruction of Earth's resources continues, *as long as* it is more profitable to make war than to make peace, *as long as* children are taught the art of killing instead of how to live peaceably with their neighbours, *as long as* it is acceptable to use child and slave labour to mollify an ever more materialistic Western society lifestyle, *as long as* it is politically expedient to use racial and religious intolerance as weapons against the innocent, *as long as* violence, fraud, deceit, gross immorality and every other evil are seen as legitimate means to create wealth, *as long as* the world's material riches remain in the hands of a privileged few and *as long as* governments in their bid for total people control, continue to systematically erode individual freedom, our materially obsessed world will continue to slide towards ultimate and inevitable anarchy. *"Those who do not learn from the past",* warns Immanuel Velikovsky in his book " Mankind In Amnesia*", are for ever condemned to relive it.*

The clock is ticking and warning world leaders that the time for change is *NOW.* If, however, for whatever reason, those in power continue along the path of inaction and corruption, then nothing but an *enforced change in human nature,* will have to occur to create *"A new heart, and a new spirit in the heart of Mankind".* The rapid decline of the once mighty Roman empire destroyed from within by moral depravity, social decadence and lawlessness is an ominous warning the rulers of this world must heed.

Whereas, from a human point of view, the outlook is bleak - the Bible gives us hope for the future. Clearly, as has been shown, today's corruption, violence and gross immorality cannot exist in the coming Kingdom of GOD when – *"All the earth shall be full of the glory of the Lord."* As Bible students watch Man's slow decline into uncontrollable anarchy, they recall Christ's warning that before His return, there would be a time of unprecedented political and social upheaval – *with no way out !* It is a time which in biblical terms is seen as a prelude to *"The Day Of The Lord" and "Armageddon".* (*Viz. Luke Ch. 21 et al*). And so, whether those in power are willing to change their priorities or not, the signs are evident – this Earth is progressively heading towards a day of final reckoning and judgment !

And in the Book of Acts, the Apostle Paul makes it clear that it will be the returned, risen Christ who will be the ultimate judge of this world.

Acts 17:31 (NKJ)

"Because He (GOD) has appointed a day in which He will judge the world in righteousness by the Man whom He has ordained. He has given assurance of this to all by raising Him from the dead."

Christ not only warned His disciples that divine reckoning would come *'as a thief in the night'* when, as in the days of Noah, the world would be too occupied with the pleasures of this life, but He also gave many clear warnings regarding the signs which would herald the Day of the Lord. As was shown earlier, in this regard, one of the most important signs is the return of the Jews to their ancient land. Not surprising then that Bible students regard the establishment of the State of Israel in 1948 as a sign as well as a warning, heralding the establishment of the Kingdom of GOD. When we consider the odds against this ancient nation surviving at all, despite thousands of years of persecution and dispersion, we cannot but marvel at the Lord's ongoing care for His people to bring them safely into the 21st Century. Nothing ,but the Jews' destined role as *'The Chosen People of the Lord'*, divinely appointed to be the *'Core Citizens'* in the coming Kingdom of GOD, can explain the continuing existence of the State of Israel and the Jewish people, still daily threatened with destruction by their Arab neighbours.

Ancient Egypt, Persia, Babylon, Assyria, the might of Rome, Nazi Germany and many others – all tried and failed in their attempt to destroy the Jews, their laws and unique culture. All these once powerful nations are long gone, but 'The People of the Lord' remain to our present day, standing at the grave sites of their persecutors - eternal witnesses and testimony to GOD's promise:

Jer. 30:11 *(NKJ)*

"Though I make an end of all nations whither I have scattered you, yet will I not make a full end of you."

A Remnant Shall Be Saved !
Youth Aliyah – Hungarian Jewish Orphaned
Children Leaving For Palestine

In the light of the foregoing exposition, we can now <u>fully</u> answer the question posed by the writer Mark Twain alluded to earlier in this section. " **What is the secret of the Jew's immortality ?**

SUMMARY

**The Jews - The Abrahamic Covenant
And The True Christian Gospel.**

I t has been shown that the Jewish people still occupy a central position in the overall purpose of GOD. However, as their own scriptures testify, this privilege is not bestowed on them as a reward for obedience, but because of their appointed role as the witnesses of GOD's power and glory and their natural descent from Abraham, the progenitor of their race. Because of his outstanding faith, the Lord made two important promises to Abraham, (later repeated to his son Isaac and grandson Jacob) regarding *(1), the everlasting possession of the Land of Israel by his descendents, the Jews and (2), a universal blessing of peace and prosperity for all (gentile) nations, centred in Abraham's 'seed' which, says the Apostle Paul, is CHRIST, the Jewish Messiah.* These promises, referred to by Paul as *'the Gospel first preached unto Abraham '*, were initially restricted to Jews, *'The Chosen People of the Lord.'* However because of their lack of faith and ultimate rejection of their Messiah, the promises were extended worldwide to include all Gentiles (non-Jews), irrespective of race, gender, colour or social status. And *this* was the Gospel, the Good News of the Kingdom of GOD preached by Jesus and the Apostles first in Israel and then throughout all the ancient world.

<u>Note:</u>* *Although the biblical references quoted in this section, have been carefully chosen to highlight the Jewish people's extraordinary ability to survive, other doctrinal aspects have not been considered, since they are outside the scope of this book. It is hoped such omissions do not detract from the importance and impact of the overall message.*

SUMMARY (Contd.)

The Apostle Paul writing to the Ephesians summarises 'The Gospel' (The Good News) as applicable to both Jews and gentiles

Eph 2:12-13 & 19 (NKJ)

"That at that time you were without Christ, being aliens from the Commonwealth of Israel and strangers from the covenants of promise, having no hope and without God in the world. 13 But now in Christ Jesus you who once were far off have been brought near by the blood of Christ. 19 Now, therefore, you are no longer strangers and foreigners, but fellow citizens with the saints   (those set apart) and members of the household of God."*

And, just as there were conditions for the Jews to be accepted as "GOD's Chosen People", so there are also three conditions for <u>both Jews and Gentiles</u> to be accepted into the Household of GOD under the Christian dispensation. They are:

1. **Because allegiance to Christ calls for a lifelong commitment, such an important decision can only be made after careful consideration by a responsible adult person.**

2. **An understanding of and belief in the Abrahamic Covenant and its practical implications on the future lifestyle of the new believer.**

3. **A publicly witnessed baptism by total immersion in water, thereby 'sealing' the believer's commitment to a new life in Christ. (Rom.Ch.6)**

(SUMMARY (Contd.)

The Ancient Kingdom Of Israel And
The Future Kingdom Of God

Although, as has been shown, any monarchy is made up of five basic 'elements', namely - *The Land, The People, The Capital City, The King and Statuary Laws* - in the ancient Kingdom of Israel, these elements were specifically chosen and set up by GOD, a condition which will again prevail in the coming worldwide Kingdom of The Lord. This will be ......

When The Lord Jesus Christ, Israel's rightful king, and the direct descendent from Abraham and King David, will rule the world in peace and justice from Jerusalem, capital of Israel, the land promised by God to Abraham, Isaac and Jacob for an everlasting possession. From this centre of world government, He will administer the divine laws for the Jewish people gathered from afar and a worldwide Gentile population grafted through baptism into the restored Commonwealth of Israel. This is the True Gospel preached by Jesus and the Apostles.

Jerusalem - The Eternal City
Future Capital Of The World

203

Teaching Israeli Jewish and Arab Youth
to live in partnership

Peace Child Israel was co-founded in 1988 by David Gordon and Yael Drouyannoff to teach coexistence using theatre and the arts. We educate for democratic values, tolerance and mutual respect. Arab and Jewish teens work with counterparts from around the country to create original dramas about coexistence. The plays, in Arabic and Hebrew, are performed for family, friends and the public at-large.

Common Effort brings Common Results

PART V

Some Final Thoughts On The Road To Forgiveness And Reconciliation

N

W E

S

The Memorials Cry Out –
To Forgive But Not To Forget

T he Berlin initiative was of course primarily intended to enable Jews who, as children, were evicted by the Nazi government, to visit the 'New City Of Berlin' and to experience for themselves, the resurgence of Jewish cultural and economic life in the capital. But for those who still have memories of Hitler's death camps, the Berlin visit is not merely a physical experience – it is also an unforgettable emotional event. For a Jew, who survived the horrors of Auschwitz, to stand at the foot of a shrine, which reca
lls the murder of his entire family, presents an unimaginable traumatic challenge - *TO FORGIVE, BUT NEVER TO FORGET.* Sadly, but very understandably, more than 60 years on, there are still some for whom the memories of the past, make anything associated with Germany simply a bridge too hard to cross, and so their emotional grief can find no rest. As shown in PART III, in many ways, the Berlin experience has to be seen as a pilgrimage of the soul – an inner struggle to reconcile the traumatic experiences of childhood with the reality of today's Germany, a nation *'spiritually reborn from the ashes of its violent past'.* This applies especially to those Jews, who even after 60 years or more after their traumatic childhood, are still held in the unrelenting grip of their past experiences. For them, the mere reality of being back in the place where the diabolical plan to exterminate all Jews was first conceived and executed, must be the saddest of experiences. And there was no disguising the fact that a deeply felt sadness of the soul had clearly left its mark on the faces of some guests who were still troubled by their childhood traumas.

The memories of some I spoke to were particularly painful. There was the lady from South America, who had come with her daughter because her husband had declined the invitation. For him, the very thought of going back to Berlin, the City where his entire family had started the terrible journey to Auschwitz, where all except himself had perished, was simply too much to bear. Others I spoke to, had already lost their partner and therefore came to the program with a close relative or friend. Another lady from America remembered how she and many other children had said 'good bye' to their parents for the last time as they stood at the Anhalter Bahnhof railway station, waiting for the

Kindertransport train to take them to England. Like so many in exile, for six long years, she had kept the hope of a reunion with her parents alive, only to discover after the war that they had been unable to escape and had perished in one of the Nazi death camps. As stated earlier, during WW II, the Anhalter Bahnhof was used by the SS as a deportation centre for sending Jews to Auschwitz and other destinations in the East. One can only speculate how many of these parents started their final journey to one of the death camps from this same railway station, even perhaps from the same platform, where they had earlier seen their children board the train for England. Our hearts must go out to all Jews who come to Berlin with such painful memories! For them, the mere decision to return to the city of their childhood must be as difficult as their inner struggle to forgive. And with such sorrow of heart, how hard it must be for them to reach out and grasp the German people's out-stretched hand yearning for forgiveness and friendship?

But time is a great healer and eventually, when the years of bitterness and hate begin to fade, the *real world* can hopefully again be seen in a more positive light. Through this program, the Berlin Senate offers to all ex-German Jews a unique opportunity to reflect on how they as individuals can make a personal contribution to the spiritual resurgence of this great City which was once their home. But undoubtedly, the greatest gift German Jews have given to this nation, and indeed the world, are *FAITH, HOPE AND LOVE* - the eternal spiritual values enshrined in their Holy Scriptures which stand for ever above Man's inhumanity to Man.

Whilst reflecting on the question of personal forgiveness, I became aware that the real significance of this program was intrinsically tied up with an indefinable '*Ultimate Purpose*' which somehow lay 'concealed' in the word '*RECONCILIATION*'. Whilst the program's daily activity sheets adequately outlined the schedule, there was little information regarding the program's *Ultimate Purpose*. In other words, whereas the question "*WHAT* are we doing today ?" was adequately addressed, answers to the question "*WHY* are we doing it" ?, seemed somewhat illusive and difficult to define. It was therefore something of a surprise, when I became aware that the '*missing link*' to this enigma was actually 'hidden' in the word "*RECONCILIATION*" itself, the very concept on which the program is based. And with this new insight, *The Ultimate Purpose* of the program became clear.

To understand this reasoning, we have to look at the root semantics of this word **RECONCILIATION**. There is here evidently a link with the word '*Re*concile', where the prefix *'RE'* implies that a '*RECIPROCAL'* action of some sort, (as for example in a handshake), is taking place between two people or a group of people. Whilst one party is the initiator, the other ' *RE*sponds' by reaching out his own hand, thereby 'completing' the action and establishing a bond between the two. But is this in fact a true indication of what the two parties are thinking? Are they *really* '*RE*conciled and are they *really* prepared to put their differences behind them, and together work towards a 'common goal'? Whilst, the handshake may be seen as the **outward** visible manifestation of that bond - it does not necessarily *RE*flect the true feelings of the two parties -because, *it is in their hearts and minds* where the *innermost feelings* about their relationship lie concealed.

When this rationale is applied to German/Jewish reconciliation, the true significance of the program initiated by the organizers' '*outstretched hand* ' takes on an entirely new meaning. Because by definition, a genuine handshake requires the participation and good will of two people, without this *RE*eciprocal action by the '*RE*ceiver', the program can only <u>partially</u> fulfil its *Ultimate Purpose*. The *RE*conciliation process is therefore not complete, <u>until and unless,</u> there is a desire on behalf of the '*RE*ceiver' to give something back in return. And that symbolic handshake has an even deeper meaning - for it is not only an expression of the Senate's bid for friendship with the visitors to the program, but also in a wider sense, the 'outstretched hand' signals a changed German attitude towards *ALL* Jews - the re-established German/Jewish communities, as well as those Jews still in the Diaspora, especially those who grew up in Germany during the Nazi era.

Furthermore, for the Jewish guests, the 'completed handshake' is also symbolic of their own acceptance of the German initiative for what it <u>really</u> is – a genuine and sincere effort by the Government and people to visibly demonstrate not only to Jews everywhere, but indeed, to the world at large, that this nation earnestly seeks forgiveness for the terrible crimes that were committed against the Jewish people and other minorities during the Nazi dictatorship.

Seen in this way, the program fulfils two important functions – **Firstly**, it acts as a 'catalyst' for the City of Berlin and indirectly for the German people themselves, to reach out to former Jewish citizens, asking their forgiveness, and **Secondly**, it is an invitation to all Jews privileged to be participants in the program, to 'grasp' that hand and to close the gap of. distrust and fear which has for so long divided German Jews and gentiles. Only, when such a mutual bond has been established _between individuals_, can the true reconciliation process begin and the _Ultimate Purpose_ of the Program be fulfilled.

But let us now look more closely at this word _'forgiveness'_. In the accepted sense, it is generally associated with religious remorse or atonement for some immoral or socially unacceptable behaviour by a person or group of persons. To be effective, forgiveness has to be a bilateral act – and as in the symbolic handshake mentioned earlier, both the perpetrator of the crime and the victim have to be involved. The former has to **_'ask'_** the victim for forgiveness and the latter has to be willing to **_'accept'_**. By its very existence, the German/Jewish Reconciliation Program testifies to the German people's changed attitude as expressed by the former Berlin Mayor, Herr Eberhard Diepgen. (_See Page 43_)

" _We Germans made a solemn vow, never to forget the crimes of the past, to live up to our responsibilities and, as far as humanly possible, to make amends for the injustices for which we have been responsible"._

But, to expect survivors who were the victims of Nazi atrocities, to forgive the German present generation, knowing that it was their parents and grandparents who committed these crimes, is by any standard, an almost impossible demand. In order to understand the process of forgiveness, we have first to look at how thought processes are created and developed in the human mind. What then is this process which shapes out thoughts and actions ? It all has to do with the mental process which creates and sustains what is known as 'Fixed Belief Systems'. When the mind is repeatedly fed with specific information, such as for instance, racial or religious propaganda, in time, this data becomes permanently 'locked' into the subconscious mind and eventually forms the basis of a 'Permanent _(fixed)_ Belief System'. Once such a 'Belief System' is _'fixed'_ in the mind, especially in the young, the ability to think rationally, i.e _'outside the square'_, and the will to investigate alternative solutions, are substantially reduced. And it is precisely this type of deliberate psychological _brainwashing'_ which lies at the root of all totalitarian and extreme religious movements. In the case of Jewish Holocaust survivors, there is often a natural, but very understandable reluctance to _'release'_ from the mind ingrained negative concepts about _'all things German being 'evil'_. Such spiritually destructive thoughts can over time become so overwhelming that the only *'perceived truth'* is that *"ALL GERMANS ARE GUILTY".*

Clearly, such a biased view is neither rational nor edifying and does little to further the reconciliation process. It is irrational because it fails to acknowledge the great positive changes which have taken place in Germany in recent years. Whilst, the responsibility for Nazi crimes committed against Jews and others by Germans and their accomplices from other lands are indisputable and must <u>never</u> be 'whitewashed', *'classifying the guilty',* has to be on a sound, realistic basis. More than 60 years after Auschwitz, it is therefore unreasonable to place **<u>all</u>** Germans living today in the *'Guilty Basket'.* This is especially so with regard to the three post-war German generations, generations yet unborn, the *'Righteous Gentiles'* and the brave resistance fighters who during WW II risked their lives helping Jews and others to survive.* The difficult process of *'personal forgiveness'* has therefore to start by mentally 'disassociating' these groups from the crimes that were committed against the Jewish people by the Nazi dictatorship. And with this new awareness, then comes the realization that ' *NOT <u>ALL</u> GERMANS ARE GUILTY '.*

The following suggestions may be helpful in furthering this process of acceptance.

1   **ACKNOWLEDGMENT** that not all Germans were or are 'guilty' and that it is no longer reasonable or just to blame three post-war generations for what happened before they were even born.

2   **RECOGNITION** that brave Germans and other nationals risked their own lives during the days of persecution by giving shelter to Jewish families or individual refugees fleeing from the Gestapo and the SS. Some of these heroes are remembered in the Avenue Of Righteous Gentiles in Jerusalem, and all Jews owe them a lasting debt.

3   **ACCEPTANCE** that Nazi brutality was not solely directed against the Jewish people, but also against German resistance fighters, Christian dissidents and others, who all fell victim to the Nazi regime because of their religious beliefs, political convictions, or racial ancestry.

I suggested earlier, that a heartfelt hand-shake between two like - minded persons symbolizes, but may not necessarily represent '*true forgiveness*', and that such a gesture of goodwill can only be 'complete' where *both* parties are freed from suspicion and fear. Although the all embracing directive '*to forgive your enemy*' lies at the very heart of Christian teaching, for an entire nation to ask forgiveness for the grievous wrong committed by them, and to openly admit in public their criminal past,is surely one of the most difficult tasks any human being or nation can be called upon to do.

That Germany, with such a barbaric history should have deliberately cho-sen to '*stand for judgment before the world'*, is from a political 'face saving' point of view, without precedent. It is therefore important that this national act of self-incrimination is recognized for what it is and seen to be more than merely a superficial or dishonest attempt to be seen to atone for Nazi atrocities against Jews and other minorities. The change that has taken place in post-war Germany goes much deeper than that and should be recognized as evidence of the people's moral courage to admit the most terrible crime in history perpetrated by their own fathers and grandfathers. Nothing could illustrate this better than the decision to place the national memorial to the six million Jewish victims of the Holocaust right in the centre of Berlin, at the very heart of where once the decision was made to exterminate the entire Jewish population of Europe.

Because the time for personal contact between Germans and the survivors of Hitler's death camps is fast running out, there is a real danger that as their numbers diminish, the terrible crimes of the Nazi era will over time be '*watered down'*, and may even in years to come be regarded by some as having been '*justified' in* the light of Israel's ongoing struggle for survival. It is therefore all the more important that the thin, but distinct demarcation line between '*,forgetting'* and '*forgiving'* does not become blurred. Though Jews who have been privileged to take part in the Reconciliation Program may find it within their heart to forgive, neither Jews nor Germans *MUST EVER FORGET* thelessons of the Holocaust memorials and what they represent. In this regard, the memorial outside the Wittenberg Underground station listing

---

Note: * *Suggested Reading : "The Last Jews Out Of Berlin"*
Leonard Gross; Carroll &Gross Publishers Inc, New York 1992

the concentration camps to which Berlin Jews were deported, is a forceful daily reminder to Berliners on their way to the office: "*These Are The Places Of Horror We Must Never Be Allowed To Forget*".(See *Page 107*)

And so the memorials for the murdered victims continue to cry out, not for vengeance, but for an end to hatred and for peace between Jews and gentiles wherever they may be, between diverse religious and ethnic groups, and between all nations. But only those whose are attuned to hear their heart wrenching cry, can comprehend the tortured lament of the dead in the silence of eternity, imploring the living to look beyond the painful past and to see these *"Sentinels Of Guilt"* not only as epitaphs of their own suffering, but also as symbols of the German peoples' *'outstretched hands'*, pleading for forgiveness.

Ultimately, however, the real significance of these memorials lies not *only* in their condemnation of Nazi brutality, but in their wider condemnation of **all** governments, who for the sake of national prestige and political expediency continue to pursue the same racial policies as the Nazi government. These memorials therefore point the finger of 'guilt' at **all** governments who still ignore the lessons of the Nazi era. For sadly, as we look at the world today - nothing has changed! Vested interests of powerful multi-national corporations, especially in the hugely profitable arms and oil industries, still dictate the military and economic policies of governments worldwide. It is indeed a sad indictment on the United Nations General Assembly that as the world's principal peace keeper, the organisation has repeatedly failed in its most important task of preventing the death of countless innocent people. The list is endless - Uganda, Cambodia, Rwanda, Kosovo, Somalia, the Belgian Congo, Korea, Vietnam, Nicaragua, Afghanistan, Iraq, Darfour and elsewhere. There is no doubt, many deaths from famine and civil wars could have been prevented, had those in power acted in unison with a concerted effort and in time. By their very existence, these German memorials therefore stand not only as silent accusers and judges over the powers which control world affairs and who, in pursuit of their own selfish interests, fail to prevent such tragedies, but they are also a warning to all future generations how easily those in power can by deceitful propaganda entice ordinary men and women to become *willing participants* in the most appalling atrocities against the innocent.

Since time immemorial, nations have cried "PEACE, PEACE" whilst preparing for, and waging war. Sadly, as we witness continued strife between nations, it seems today's politicians have learnt nothing from the past. They do not understand the true meaning of 'Peace', and in reality only seek a cessation of hostilities *on their own terms*. 'Peace' -**REAL** Peace, is not merely a matter of laying down arms - it can only come from a *morally driven commitment to cease aggression* – to place 'human lives ahead of political expediency, to seek compromise, not conflict and to honour the dignity of all people. True Peace is a spiritual, not a secular attribute and like true reconciliation between former enemies, can only come from *'a change of the heart'*. In the German context, that change of heart is not only evident in this reconciliation program, but also in the generally more tolerant attitude of the people towards the less privileged in their society. In this regard, it is encouraging that many Jewish and German organisations have for years been working together in an atmosphere of mutual trust and respect. A 2005 article in the magazine Aktuell *(76 / 2005)* shows that there are now no less than 30 such groups in Germany actively promoting German/Jewish friendship. Whilst for the survivors, recognition and acceptance of this change of heart in the German people is an important first step, for the former aggressor, whoever he may be, the first milestone on the difficult road to reconciliation has, as in Germany, to be a sincere admission of guilt, followed by practical efforts to make amends for the past. On both counts, the Berlin program, successive German governments and many individuals have aptly fulfilled these criteria and have by their efforts, placed both Jews and gentiles on the road to a better understanding and mutual respect - the ONLY road which in the end leads to true reconciliation.

When however, a national government and its people deliberately set out to exterminate an entire race, be it for ethnic, religious, or other reasons – no act of atonement can adequately compensate the victims for their suffering. *It may be the time to forgive, but never to forget!* For what the Nazi government did to the Jewish people in the years from 1933 to 1945, and for the willingness of the vast majority of Germans to blindly follow that evil regime willingly and with enthusiasm, not all the tears of grief shed by the survivors in remembrance of those who perished, nor the tears of remorse shed by the descendants of those who committed these crimes, can ever express the sorrow and suffering experienced by the Jewish people during the years of the Nazi dictatorship.

BUT TEARS ARE NOT ENOUGH !

But however painful, the negative past must not be allowed to dominate the thinking of future generations for ever. There must come a time when both the perpetrator of the crime and victim have 'to move forward'. That time is now! Today, with worldwide Internet, email, mobile and fax technology, opportunities abound, as never before, for every new generation of German and Jewish youth to grasp each others' hand - '*to close the gap', and in the spirit of the Plötzensee Memorial, to accept each other on equal terms as members of the same human family*. As a founder member of the European Union, a remarkable change of heart has taken place in recent years in this country and it is now the young men and women in each new generation who have to build on the foundation left by earlier generations. In this regard, the already well established German/Israeli friendship offers a sound basis for continuing Jewish /Christian dialogue.

Thanks to modern technology, young people everywhere can now look beyond the negative influences which in the past have created distrust and fear, to a future where the lives of their children, grandchildren and generations yet unborn may grow up together without fear and suspicion. By continuing to support Jewish communities, the German people have brought true reconciliation between Jew and Gentile a little closer, and it is on this '*rebirth of the soul'* that the future success of German/Jewish relations will ultimately be judged.

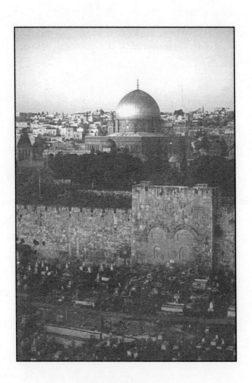

The Golden Gate

The Mercy (Golden) Gate (Bab el Rahmeh) appears in the legends of three religions - Judaism, Christianity and Islam. An early Jewish tradition holds that it is through this gate that the Messiah will enter Jerusalem. According to Christian tradition, Jesus made his last entry to Jerusalem through the Mercy Gate. The Muslims refer to it as the Gate of Mercy and believe it to be the gate referred to in the Koran, through which the just will pass on the Day of Judgment

PART VI
Epilogue

THE BEITH HAGEFEN JEWISH / ARAB PEACE INITIATIVE
OBJECTIVES OF THE ORGANISATION

To eliminate and minimize stereotype thinking and generalization; To initiate personal acquaintance between Jews and Arabs; To emphasize what is common to Jews and Arabs citizens of the State of Israel by using Arts, Music and Drama to enhance education toward tolerance and peace.

Overall View of the Peace Garden Complex

A Study Class of Arab and Israeli Children at Beith Hagefen

218

EPILOGUE

W hen, in September 2000, after our unforgettable week in Berlin, I first decided to write a report about that experience, little did I know that what started out as a script of only a few pages, would more than six years later be published in America as a fully illustrated book with 235 pages. That long journey into my own past and that of other survivors has not been an easy one! The sheer effort of trying to relive my own childhood and that of Jews, who actually experienced the horror of Hitler's death camps, some of whom had lost their entire families in the Nazi Holocaust, was often an emotionally draining and sometimes even tearful experience. It all began when in early 2001, the initial manuscript was distributed to a limited number of readers in Australia, Germany and England under the title: *'A Visit To The New Berlin'*. However, from readers' comments and suggestions received, it soon became clear that a book with a title more appropriate to the contents would attract a wider readership. And so, in 2002 work began on the present book *" Tears Are Not Enough -The German Jewish Reconciliation Program faces the Truth about the Nazi Holocaust"*. Depending on demand, *this* work may at a later stage also be made available on the Internet and as a CD. Extensive research, countless hours on the computer, pernicious computer viruses and unending technical problems, delays with overseas copyright permission, to say nothing of problems following major back surgery and twice moving house, often made the work seem like a never ending task. Nevertheless, despite many delays, from 2003, work on the manuscript continued steadily and in September 2006, the first copies finally came off the press at the American publisher. Within 6 months, all copies from the first printing were sold out and a 2nd printing was initiated with an Indian publisher known to the author.

Because *"Tears Are Not Enough"* addresses reconciliation from different perspectives in an unbiased manner, it will most likely appeal to Jewish and Christian readers as well as members of various ethnic communities. Furthermore, the successful, long-term operation of this German initiative, may also provide helpful guidelines to government departments and similar organizations when dealing with specific problems regarding reconciliation.

Primarily, however, this book is of course intended for Jewish readers, familiar with the history of pre-war Berlin and for past participants in the German program, as well as Jews in the Diaspora who have not yet availed themselves of this unique program and may after reading the book be moved to participate in this 'once in a lifetime experience'. In addition, it is hoped other readers will have found the information on early Australian colonial settlement and its effect on this country's indigenous population of interest. Also, the outline of pre-war German history is relevant, as even today, the historical past in both the Federal Republic and Australia still influences government attitudes towards reconciliation. It is perhaps not even unreasonable to assume that similar constraints as those in Australia, also apply in Canada and the United States with their own native populations.

But, beyond this, it is hoped that what is written here, can lead to a better all-round understanding between individual members of different races, religions and ethnic backgrounds, wherever they may be. By its practical demonstration of *'reaching out to the other side'*, of encouraging trust and respect between former enemies, the German program can be regarded as a useful blueprint for dealing with a wide range of problems associated with ethnic communities. As has been shown here, the impetus behind the Program's message, lies <u>*not*</u> in what it provides in purely material terms to those who participated, but in what it **morally represents** by its very existence and successful long-term operation.

As the German experience shows, effective reconciliation cannot be achieved simply by political rhetoric, financial compensation or legislation. Reconciliation between peoples of diverse cultures, religions and ethnic backgrounds can be neither effective nor long lasting, unless it is seen by <u>both</u> sides as **'A Matter Of The Heart'**. The seeds of mutual trust and respect can therefore only grow where, as in post-war Germany, there is strong political will by governments to change established, often deeply entrenched norms and attitudes and most importantly, where there is a genuine resolve by all parties to treat *'the other side'* with dignity and respect as members of the same human family.

But the message the German program presents to the world, does not only address governments and organisations. Even as the breaching of the Berlin Wall in 1989 became a symbol for freedom of the oppressed worldwide, so this Reconciliation Program also sends its message of hope to the millions who still face daily persecution in many lands because of their race and/or religious beliefs. Most remarkable is the fact that this program originated in the country where the unspeakable crimes associated with the Nazi Holocaust were planned and initiated. The very fact that it came into being at all, is a measure of the changed government attitude regarding Jews and other minorities which has taken place in post-war German thinking. Based on the German model, organisations responsible for reconciliation between people of diverse ethnic and religious background can now approach their work from a new perspective. Although, as the Australian experience indicates, there is still a long way to go, as shown in PART I, there are nevertheless many areas where significant progress has been made. Moreover, looking further afield, it is encouraging to see that an increasing number of countries attracted by the social and political rewards of greater public participation in the national decision making process, are now beginning to examine the benefits of a democratically elected governance. Even some countries from the former Soviet communist block and Middle East Arab states seem now to be slowly moving towards a politically less restrictive form of government. But it is the humanitarian organisations like World Vision, Care, Save the Children Fund, Oxfam, Green Peace and many others who through their untiring efforts to bridge the gap between the '*Haves*' and the '*Have Nots*' of this world who are the pioneers at the forefront of a global movement to create a better future for *all* future generations, irrespective of colour, race or religion. It is this author's sincere wish that what is written here, may in some small way contribute towards achieving that end.

THE BERLIN MEMORIAL TO THE 6,000,000
MURDERED EUROPEAN JEWS

When we visited Berlin in September 2000, much of the Eastern sector, the former DDR, was still a barren wasteland. In the area between the Reichstag building and the Brandenburger Tor, stood a large structure marking the site where the national memorial to the 6,000,000 European Jews murdered by the Nazi government, was to be erected. (*See Page 93*), In May 2005, soon after the 60th. Anniversary marking the end of WW II, that memorial, designed by the American architect Peter Eisenmann, was finally opened to the public by the then Bundespresident Wolfgang Thierse. It is not only intended to be a place of remembrance, but also a retreat for quiet contemplation. Most importantly however, this memorial is a permanent reminder to Germany and in a wider sense to all world governments of how a nation, renowned for its cultural heritage, yet obsessed with the bid for world domination, set out from this place in 1933, to commit the greatest crime in history – the planned extermination of 11,000,000 European men, women and children whose only crime was that they were Jews.

But, sixty years on, looking beyond the historical and political factors which led to this monstrous crime, it is important to recognise the profound change of heart which has taken place in the German nation. There is therefore great significance in the decision to deliberately erect this 19,000 SM memorial at the very heart of the capital in the country where this unimaginable crime against humanity was initiated. Also, to place this memorial on the same site where for 28 years stood the infamous Berlin Wall, symbol of a divided nation, is of great significance because, in a very real sense this cenotaph to Man's inhumanity to Man forms a 'spiritual bridge' between the negative past of the former Nazi Germany and Communist domination on the one hand, and, the present German democratic Federal Republic on the other. Here, where East meets West in a united effort to rebuild the nation, the soul reaches out in hope to build on the lessons learnt from the past.

Note: completion date was scheduled for 2003 but actual inauguration was not until in May 2005).

There is no designated entrance or exit to the site, allowing visitors to enter from all directions and to find their 'spiritual balance' among the 2711 stone blocks which vary in height from 30 centimetres to almost 5 meters, giving the illusion of an undulating sea when viewed from above.

But as one proceeds along the narrow, undulating tile paths, surrounded by huge 'lifeless' granite blocks of varying height, deep in one's own thoughts contemplating the enormity of what this memorial represents in terms of the greatest of all Man-made tragedies, any sense of physical reality is overtaken by a heart-rending feeling of *'being irretrievably lost in a hostile environment'*. And this is exactly what this place of remembrance is intended to convey - the utter sense of spiritual and physical misery and hopelessness experienced by the thousands of Jews as they were being mass transported in cattle wagons to the death camps. Above all, this memorial expresses the most profound of all human emotions -the feeling of being totally forgotten and *'lost'* in the world and having nowhere to turn to for love. The fact that there are no inscriptions on the blocks, no epitaphs to individual murdered Jews, adds a sense of surreal anonymity to the scene and gives the same feeling of *'nameless non-entity'* experienced by the inmates of concentration camps, whose family identity had been *'obliterated'* and replaced with numbers tattooed on their arm. Making Jews a 'non-entity', was a deliberate Nazi attempt to squeeze the last drop of self esteem and human dignity out of their victims. These numbers were then recorded in the American IBM record system with specific letter codes designating the ultimate fate of individual prisoners. Depending on which 'square' on the card was punched, determined whether the victim was to be shot, gassed or used for medical experiments. Whilst, strict SS records were kept for those prisoners destined for slave labour and medical experiments, virtually no official records were kept for the sick, the old and the dying destined on arrival for the gas chambers. As mentioned previously, the SS considered these wretches of humanity to be merely 'vermin' and their lives were totally irrelevant to the Nazi system. On arrival at Auschwitz, all deportees were segregated and classified as either *'useful'* or *'useless'*. *(See Page 104)*. Whilst those taken to the right were to be used as slave labour in quarries and factories attached to the camps, the old, the young and the infirm were directed to the left, destined to be shot or for immediate extermination in the gas chambers.

In an underground chamber below the memorial, in "The Room Of Names", set up with the help of the Jerusalem Holocaust Memorial

Centre Yad Vashem, an audio and visual presentations partly based on former SS records, give back to victims of the Nazi terror at least some of their identity, and human dignity.

THE BERLIN MEMORIAL TO THE 6,000,000 MURDERED EUROPEAN JEWS

Although, ***writing "Tears Are Not Enough"***, has often been a journey of sad memories, it has also been a journey of hope and it could not have happened without the long-term support of many German Gentiles and Jews, most of whom are unknown to this author. These are the 'unsung heroes' who together committed their effort and time to this unique and worthy cause of bringing former Jews back to Berlin and other German cities from the lands of their dispersion. there, in the city of their birth these ageing Jews, now mostly in their 70s and 80s, came to experience for themselves '*A Nation Spiritually Reborn Out Of The Ashes Of The Past' It is* therefore fitting that this book should end with a positive vision of the coming Kingdom of GOD on Earth ,- an image of the future, looking forward to a time

---

When *"They shall beat their swords into ploughshares, and their spears into pruning hooks; when nation shall not lift up sword against nation, neither shall they learn war any more -. for out of Zion shall go forth the law, and the Word of the Lord from Jerusalem.* **Isaiah Ch. 2:4**

When *"They shall not hurt nor destroy in all my holy mountain: for the earth shall be full of the knowledge of the Lord, as the waters cover the sea."* **Isaiah Ch.11:9**

When *" Everyone shall sit under his vine and under his fig tree, and no one shall make them afraid; for the mouth of the Lord of hosts has spoken it."* **Micah Ch .4:4**

When *God will wipe away every tear from their eyes; there shall be no more death, nor sorrow, nor crying. There shall be no more pain, for the former things have passed away."* **Rev 21:4**

I close this book then with a final expression of my grateful thanks to the former Governing Mayor, Herr Eberhard Diepgen, the program organizers and the many others people who by their ongoing support, have made this unforgettable Berlin experience possible for so many Jews who, as children, became the innocent victims of the Nazi terror. It is my earnest wish that as the program continues to grow, all the Jewish guests who have been privileged to share in this venture, will return to their homeland as the program's most enthusiastic ambassadors, confident in the knowledge that with the continued goodwill of the Senate and the German people, the future well being of Berlin's Jewish Communities is assured

BERLIN

PART VII

APPENDIX

Bibliography
Photo Acknowledgements
Suggested Reading

ACKNOWLEDGEMENTS

Some of the photographs in this book have been obtained from various published books and magazines © as indicated below. All other photos not listed, were either taken by the author during the Berlin visit or were obtained from private sources. A comprehensive list of all photos is given on pages ix –x.

The bitmaps made with Macromedia™, Macromedia Inc. are produced by kind permission from Nodtronics Pty. Ltd. 2000, Australia

All Bible references are taken from the CD disc 'The PC Study Bible ©Thomas Nelson Inc. , The Holy Bible-the New King James Version of the Bible © Thomas Nelson Inc.

The quotation from Elpis Israel by Dr. John Thomas on page 171 is from Elpis Israel © First published 1849, page 475, 15th Edition. Reproduced by kind permission of the Christadelphian Magazine & Publishing Association. Ltd, Birmingham UK.

Where photos have been directly downloaded from specific Internet websites, the author wishes to express his grateful thanks for this material which is important in supporting the message of peace "Tears Are Not Enough:" sets out to convey.

BIBLIOGRAPHY AND
PHOTO ACKNOWLEDGEMENTS

Where appropriate references are quoted in the text. The page numbers in italics refer to this book not to those of the source.

Legend: tl = Top Left; tr = Top Right; cl = Centre Left; cr =Centre Right; bl = Bottom Left; br = Bottom Right ;

Berlin Aktuell Magazine (Various 1998-2007)
Publisher Presse & Informationsdienst des Landes Berlin, D -10871;

INTRODUCTION

Page xvii, Translated excepts from a speech by Bundespräsident
Dr.Roman Herzog „Die Zukunft der Erinnerung" ; Aktuell Vol.63 / 1999

Page xx -Jüdisches Leben in Berlin. Ein Immerwährender Kalender
Haude & Spener Verlagsbuchhandlung GmbH, Berlin

PART I

Page 3   Aktuell Vol.69 / 2002
Page 4   Stiftung Jüdisches Museum, Berlin

PART II

Page 24b   Aktuell Vol.67 / 2001
Page 31,39   Aktuel Vol.64/ 1999

Page 24t   Website : www.galaxy-ritz.de/
Page 34   Website: www.adnkronos.com/aki.....
Page 34b   Website : www.antisemitism.org.il/....
Page 38   Website : http://medienkritik.typepad.com/....

Page 32r   Jüdisches Leben in Berlin. Ein Immerwährender
Page 33tl ,b   Kalender; Haude & Spener Verlagsbuch-handlung,

Page 32l, 33t Die Nazis -Eine Warnung der Geschichte LRees,1997
               Translated from the English; Diana Verlag Munich

Page 33bl,   Berlin with Potsdam with 135 Photographs (2000 ?)
Page 40   Schöning & Co.Gebr. Schmidt Lübeck V. Schickus Vertrb

PART III

Page 115b, 116t   Aktuell Vol.63 / 1999
Page 126, 146,149t   Aktuell Vol.66 / 2000
Page 149t, 150   Aktuell Vol.66 / 2000
Page 149b   Aktuell Vol.68 / 2001
Page 118tl, 119   Aktuell Vol.69 / 2002
Page 54b, 129br   Aktuell Vol.70 / 2002
Page 130   Aktuell Vol.76 / 2006
Page 105t, bl   Aktuell Vol.79 / 2000

Page 70   Die Nazis -Eine Warnung der Geschichte

Page 83   Plötzensee Memorial Centre 1996, Visitor's Commemo-
           rativeBrochure; Brigitte Oleschinski;
           The German Resistance Memorial Centre, Berlin

PART III (Contd.)

Page 84b - Jüdisches Leben in Berlin. Ein Immerwährender Kalender
Page 100 Haude & Spener Verlagsbuchhandlung GmbH, Berlin
Page 105br Ibid
Page 116 Ibid
Page 117br Ibid

Page 96 German Embassy, London UK;Berlin Holocaust Memorial
Webssite: http://www.german -embassys.org.uk/holocaust

Page 100b Jüdische Stätten in Berlin, Bill Rebiger, B.Jaron Verlag
Page 113b GmbH,Auflage 2000

Page 53 Berlin with Potsdam with 135 Photographs -2000
Page 110l Schöning & Co.Gebr. Schmidt Lübeck V. SchickusVertrieb
Page 55bl, br Ibid
Page 56 Ibid
Page 57 Ibid
Page 78 Ibid
Page 118t Ibid

Page 60t,bl Joachim Mahrzahn 1992 ; Staatliche Museen Vorder-
asiatisches Museum zu Berlin Verlag PhllippVon Zapern
Mainz

Page 66 Microsoft Encarta 2005; © Microsoft Corporation Inc.
All rights reserved

Page 114bl Unterm Hakenkreuz 1933 -1945; Presse Und Informationsamt der Stadt Frankfurt/Main

Page135 Waldschule Kaliski, Berlin Dahlem Brochure 1938
Page137,138 Ibid
Insel der Geborgenheit? Die private Waldschule Kaliski
Berlin 1932 bis 1939 (Gebundene Ausgabe) Hertha L.
Busemann ,Michael Daxner ,Werner Fölling Verlag:

Page 172 Commander Of The Exodus, Jossie Harel & Joram, Kaniuk
Grove Press Books-distributed by Publishers Group West,
New York, USA
Page 174 (Quotation)

PART III (Contd.)

Page 180   Elpis Israel–Dr.JohnThomas; First published1849
               Christadelphian Magazine & Publishing Association. Ltd,
               Birmingham England (Quotation from p.475)

Page 99	Website: http://history1900s.about.com/
Page 118b	Website: http://www.personal.umrich.edu/
Page 120t	Website: http://news.google.com.au/
Page140,166	Website: http://travel.webshots.com/
Page 181	Website: http://images.google.com.au/
Page 104r,200	Website: http://motic.learning center.wiesenthal.org/
Page 194	Website: http://www.flickr.com/
Page 203, 216	Website: http://www.google.com.au/
Page 204	Website: http://mideastweb.org/peacechild/
Page 218	Website: http://www.beithhagefen.com/
Page 224	Website: http:/www.secret-destinations.com/

SUGGESTED FURTHER READING

N o other subject, except the Bible, has been so extensively researched and written about than the Nazi Holocaust. Through countless works of writers, historians and survivors from the Nazi death camps, millions of readers worldwide have relived the Nazi era and especially all aspects of the terror that was Hitler's 'Final Solution Program' for the Jews of Europe. The books listed below are a selection from the author's private library and recommended for further reading.

The Last Jews In Berlin; Leonard Gross
First Carrol & Graf Edition © First Carrol & Graf Publishers Inc. NY 1992

Into The Arms Of Strangers 2001;
Stories of the Kindertransport Mark Jonathan Harris & Deborah Oppenheimer
© Bloomsbury Publishing Co. London 2000

Schindler's List; Thomas Keneally
© Serpentine Publishing Co Ltd.London 1982

The Boys; The Story Of 732 Young Concentration Camp Survivors
© Martin Gilbert1996 ; Henry Holt & Co. Inc

Unterm Hakenkreuz; Frankfurt 1933-1945
© *Presse Und Informationsdienst der Stadt Frankfurt/Main 1999*

Commander Of The Exodus; Yoram Kaniuk
© *Yoram Kaniuk; Press New York 1999*

Die Nazis – Eine Warnung Der Geschichte; Laurence Rees
© *Laurence Rees; Diana Verlag Munich & Zürich 1997*

Never Again – A History Of The Holocaust; Martin Gilbert
© *Harper Collins 2000*

If This Is A Man –And The Truce; Primo Levy
Penguin Books 1995 ;© New Statesman 1971

Assimilation, Verfolgung und Exil-Am Beispiel der jüdischen Schüler eines Frankfurter Gymnasiums
©*Petra Bonavita (Mg); Schmetterling Verlag Stuttgart 2002*
All Rights Reserved; GuS-Druck,Stuttgart;Binden:IDUPA,Owen/Teck

Die Kindertransporte 111938-1939; Rettung und Integration 2002
Claudio Curio und Andrea Hammel © Fischer Taschenbuch Verlag in der S.Fischer Verlag GmbH Frankfurt/Main 20034

The Burden Of Guilt-A Short History Of Germany 1914-1945
© *Hannah Vogt;; New York/Oxford University Press 1964*

Wall Street And The Rise Of Hitler - Anthony C. Sutton ;
The Collusion Between The Nazi Government And American Big Business.
©*Anthony C. Sutton; Bloomfield Books, Suffolk , England*

Eichmann – The Savage Truth; Comer Clarke
Comer Clarke (London) Ltd. 1960

I Came Alone – The Stories Of The Kindertransport
© Ed. Bertha Leverton & Schmuel Lowensohn 1990 reprinted 1991
Publ: The Book Guild Ltd.,25 High Str., Lewes, Sussex.